YELLOWSTONE &
TETON NATIONAL PARKS

INCLUDING

JACKSON HOLE, WYOMING

BY
JOY M. JOHNSON

Published by
Spirit Dance Publishing
P.O. Box 25036
Jackson, Wy 83001 USA
Tele: (904) 735-0060

Please send all comments, corrections, additions or critiques to:
Joy M. Johnson
c/o Spirit Dance Publishing
P.O. Box 25036
Jackson Hole, Wy 83001
If you would like to offer suggestions or advice that would make a visit more enjoyable for someone else, please write to the above address. If we use it in any future revision of this book, we will include you name, city and state.

Some photos and illustrations are used by permission and are the property of the original copyright owners.
Maps by Timothy Johnson

Library of Congress Catalog Number: 93-60623
ISBN: 1-880782-14-6

Johnson, Joy M., 1959-
Includes index

Although every effort has been made to assure accuracy of information at the time of this book's printing, the publisher does not assume and hereby disclaims any liability caused by omissions, errors, or any potential travel disruption, whether such omissions or errors result from negligence, accident or any other cause.

ACKNOWLEDGEMENTS

Few books are written without the advice and help of others. I'd especially like to thank my best friend, mentor and hiking companion, Tim Johnson and my new son, Zachariah. I'd like to thank The Yellowstone and Teton National Park Services and Yellowstone Chief Historian, Jim Peaco. Special thanks to artist Chuck Ren and Greystone Press for the use of *"Wilderness Child."* I am grateful to Bessie Yarbrough for her support and encouragement and I'd also like to thank Gary Yarbrough, who taught me a valuable lesson about staying on the trail.

Dedicated to

Timothy
You make all things possible.

CONTENTS

Activities in the Parks and Jackson

Water, Water, Everywhere!

Jackson Hole, Wyoming

Area Attractions

"There are no words that can tell
the hidden spirit of the wildreness,
that can reveal its mystery,
its melancholy
and its charm."

Teddy Roosevelt

PREFACE

You are visiting the valley of Jackson Hole and the two national parks for which this valley is famous. Perhaps you know everything that you'd like to do and see during your visit. More than likely you need more information, which is why you have this guide. For any omissions or errors, I sincerely apologize. While this guide provides thousands of pieces of facts and solid information, things change; businesses move, telephone numbers change, opening and closing times and dates of the parks and businesses are inconsistent and new roads are being constructed as this book is being written.

As I have read and proofed this manuscript, I realize that a few more facts about the valley might be helpful.

First and foremost, I believe there isn't another place more beautiful or inspiring than Jackson Hole. After visiting here in 1988, I decided to make this unique and diverse valley my home. I have lived in the valley, on and off, for over 5 years. Although I now make my permanent home in Santa Fe, New Mexico, I visit the valley every excuse I get. When my travel and work projects lead me away from Jackson Hole, I frequently find myself daydreaming about this remote country. The valley's sculptured mountain ranges punctuating moody skies that also hold the brightest stars and the blackest nights imaginable or its narrow roads winding through green velvet pastures, instill a sense of pastoral tranquility like few other places can.

For me, to leave the valley is often an exercise in sensory deprivation. The feeling seems to be a mutual one. Many of the valley's people will tell you that "I only came for the skiing" or "we were only going to stay a week, but we decided we didn't want to leave." It's no wonder. But leave we must. It becomes more and more obvious every year that if the surrounding wilderness and its inhabitants are to survive, we must harden our hearts and move on. As this valley's population increases, so do clashes with nature. The natural wonders of this area **are** perishable. As urbanization spreads each passing year, from tenacious landowners and commercial exploiters, the valley experiences more pollution of the lakes, rivers, land and air. As land prices go up in value, second and third generation residents who have spent their entire lives in this valley have had to move away to more affordable communities to make way for wealthy semi-residents, who purchase large tracts of valuable land for use solely as summer retreats and ski-junkets. (Only 3% of Teton County is available for private use.) Only by providing an atmosphere of preservation, nurture and protection can we insure that future generations still find this valley to be a place of wonder and mystery, that *belongs to everyone.*

11

Lastly, the valley of Jackson Hole is not a theme park, even though some special interest groups have dedicated enormous amounts of money and planning to make the town appear so. Instead, it is a living, thriving community comprised of over 13,000 citizens throughout Teton County. Their lifestyles are very similar to your own. They work, (many in the tourist industry,) go to school and participate in community activities. In other words, Jackson Hole is their home and they welcome you. During the summer season, nearly 100,000 people at any given time are lodging, shopping, sight-seeing, dining and playing in the tiny communities throughout the valley. While the majority of citizens of Jackson Hole are eager to make your impression of their home a favorable one, a little thoughtfulness goes a long way. Remember, the streets of the Town Square are designed for automobile traffic. Stepping off curbs without checking for traffic or snapping pictures from the middle of the streets can be more than annoying; it can be dangerous.

The parks are living and thriving communities as well. An important rule of thumb here is the oft' used saying, "If you pack it in, pack it out." Nothing disrupts a stroll through pristine wilderness more quickly than a discarded soda can or disposable diaper.

What have I left out? I hope you will let me know. I encourage the readers of this guide to write with any suggestions, stories or advice that other visitors would like to know about. I will be happy to print them, along with your name, city and state in any future revisions of this book.

Welcome to Jackson Hole and the national parks. I hope you have a wonderful time!

"A thousand Yellowstone
wonders are calling,
'Look up
and down
and all around you!'"

-John Muir, 1909

YELLOWSTONE
NATIONAL PARK

YELLOWSTONE
Introduction

Although Yellowstone National Park reveals its beauty and diversity to more than 3.5 million people each year, it is still an amazing wonder even to those who come back again and again. If your impression of Yellowstone is a forested park with a few grizzlies, crowds of visitors and Old Faithful erupting in the distance, you'll be in for an unexpected surprise. Imagine more than 2,000,000 acres of alpine wilderness, thunderous waterfalls, hot springs, colorful canyons, rugged mountain peaks and wide-open valleys. Yellowstone is indeed the greatest show on earth.

Our oldest and largest national park in the lower 48 sits in the northwest corner of Wyoming, edging into Idaho and Montana. It is 63 miles in length by 54 miles wide. Here the geysers thunder, the hot springs bubble, the canyon shimmers in ocher, yellow, brown and pink and the rivers roar and tumble along peaceful, mossy banks.

Mother Nature, seemingly aware of the fragile environment that exists on this high, rolling plateau, offered her maternal protection by creating a natural buffer to enclose this magnificent area. Huge mountain ranges surround the park in the shape of a protective embrace; more than 40 peaks topping 10,000 feet or higher. The most awesome range is the Teton Mountain Range rising 13,000 feet just to the south of the park.

Since the birth of this nations first national park in 1872, man has also recognized the perilousness of an island wilderness reserve adrift in a sea of development and has sought to protect the park's natural buffers. The buffer that nature so graciously provided, man has wisely sought to permanently preserve: The Greater Yellowstone Ecosystem, some 14 million acres in all, contains two national parks, seven national forests, three wildlife refuges and one Indian reservation.

The magnificent landscape also nurtures one of the most successful wildlife sanctuaries in the world. It is impossible for you to visit the park without seeing some of the wildlife that makes Yellowstone famous. From thunderous herds of bison to thousands of elk, from big-horn sheep to trumpeter swans, from the foraging moose to the majestic grizzly - you are about to experience one of the most astounding wildlife habitats in the world.

Packs of wolves once inhabited Yellowstone, along with other predators such as the cougar and mountain lion, but a predator-killing campaign wiped them out by the early 1900's. In 1991, after many years of debate, it has been decided that the wolfs' rightful place is in Yellowstone and efforts are now being made to reintroduce the wolf to the park. The cougar is still rarely seen in Yellowstone. It's still yet to be seen if this secretive species will assume its old role in the wild. Today, management recognizes the errors of the past and seeks to restore Yellowstone to its previous state of wild enchantment for all of nature's species. There are refuges which see to the successful breeding of trumpeter swans, surrogate parenting of the whooping crane and the feeding and care of elk.

Yellowstone's lakes and streams are home to more than 16 species of fish including the native cutthroat trout, grayling, whitefish, and several different types of trout. Soaring along the mountain tops, you'll see hawks, falcons, whooping cranes, trumpeter swans, bald and golden eagles, pheasants, ducks and geese. Scurrying along the rolling moraines and along the grassy river banks you'll spot beaver, red and gold-mantled ground squirrels, chipmunks, marmots, rabbits and porcupines.

Within the park is a 142 mile long figure-eight road that links all the major points of interests. The idea to link all major points of interest with a convenient roadway system was first conceived by army engineer Daniel C. Kingman in 1886 to... "allow tourists to visit the principal points of interest without retracing their steps." While Kingman successfully linked the wonders of Yellowstone with his figure eight loop, I'm certain he never anticipated the choked roadways of today during peak tourist season. Visitors love Yellowstone, and they show up in droves each year to prove it. During mid-summer, tourists will clog the small arteries of the park in whale-sized RVs, tour busses, and tens of thousands of automobiles. At times, traffic comes to a stand-still while hordes of camera-clicking tourists snap excitedly away at a befuddled bison lumbering across the road. Hotel and lodging accommodations are often booked weeks or even months in advance and parking at many facilities will be full to capacity. However, visitors to the Yellowstone region tend to be fair-weather friends; here for the splendor of summer and gone by the crisp days of autumn. If you can avoid travel between Labor Day and mid-September, do. You'll be blessed with a feeling of quiet solitude, trails with nary a soul in sight plus the added bonus of slightly reduced off-season rates at most hotel and lodging facilities. If not, bring along plenty of patience, expect delays and traffic, and you can still experience a rewarding slice of America's "crown jewel."

HISTORY

The Yellowstone region has been inhabited by Native Americans for the past 10,000 years. Ever since the last of the earth's ice ages released its glacial grip, American Indians foraged throughout this wondrous region. Clovis and Folsom points, dating back 10 millennia and associated with bison and mammoth kills have been found in Gardiner, slightly north of the park and the Gros Ventre Mountains, just south of Yellowstone.

By about 5,000 B.C. giant bison and mammoth disappeared from the entire mid-continent. Though the cause is not fully known, possibilities include an extreme climate change or over-hunting to extinction by early man. Whatever the reason, big game was gone and the plains became baked by heat and drought. Out of necessity, hunters modified their hunting habits for the pursuit of smaller game. Elk, deer and rabbit were plentiful in the higher plateau regions such as Yellowstone and many tribes moved to this lush, green region to escape the barrenness of their old territories. About 1,000 B.C. the climate became more moderate and the herds of buffalo and elk reestablished themselves in the interior plains outside Yellowstone. Again, man adapted to these climatic changes and Yellowstone became less a haven and more of a meeting ground for early tribes who traveled there for obsidian or other resources unavailable in other regions.

By 1800 the area was most populated by the Crow, Blackfeet and Shoshone tribes, however the only permanent residents of Yellowstone were the Sheepeater Indians; a blend of the Shoshone and Bannock tribes. The Sheepeaters were considered a timid and simple tribe who hunted the bighorn sheep of this area, hence the name. They never made use of the horse since they were less nomadic than other tribes and were, therefore, considered backward and rather mysterious by the first trappers to see them.

The first map with the word "Yellowstone" printed on it was made in 1798 by the Lewis and Clark Expedition. However, Lewis and Clark had no details of what lay within the interior of the park, only that there was a "considerable falls" on the Yellowstone River, told to them by Indians of the region. The name Yellowstone is apparently derived from the Sioux name for the area, "Yellow Rock River," called so because of the yellow canyon walls and bluffs along the Yellowstone River.

Though trapper and explorer John Colter was probably the first white man to witness some of the areas wonders and peculiarities, he was called a liar by most because of the bizarreness of his tales. Yellowstone remained unmapped and unexplored by an official investigation until 1859, when a small military expedition under the command of Captain M. F. Raynolds set out for Yellowstone in the deep of winter. They were never able to penetrate its interior region due to the heavy snows and their exploration of the park was confined to its northern region.

The party that received the most acclaim and recognition for the exploration and mapping of Yellowstone was the 1871 Hayden Expedition. This expedition consisted of 34 men, a calvary escort, photographer William H. Jackson and painter Thomas Moran. By 1872 a bill was introduced, supported by the articles and speeches provided by the Hayden Expedition, to preserve and protect this unique area. It was quickly signed into law shortly thereafter by President Ulysses S. Grant and our first national park was established.

Expeditions, prospectors, hunters and tourism flourished from this point on. Travel into the park was rugged, usually by horse, wagon or stagecoach with excursions typically lasting about five days. In 1915 the automobile was introduced to Yellowstone and made travel around this region much swifter, though the average speed limit was set at 12 miles per hour.

With this influx of tourists, upgraded facilities began sprouting up under the newly created National Park Service. Forty six camps were constructed in all (only 12 of which are still standing today) to fulfill the new park service's dream of a "tourist's paradise." Clearly, the focus of the park service during that time was on visitation, rather than preservation.

This was a very difficult and confusing time for the national park concept. It was not the philosophy of man at the time to leave things in their natural state and many atrocities were committed for the sake of "taming the wild." The animals of the park were divided into two categories; "the "good" and the "bad." The "bad" species were of course predatory animals such as the wolf, grizzly, and mountain lion. These animals were hunted nearly to the point of extinction. Bear cubs were chained to posts outside the park's hotels. Elk were captured and placed in zoo-like pens for the amusement of the visitor.

Yellowstone held the last wild herd of mountain bison left anywhere, all others having already been slaughtered decades earlier. However, even the bison in the park came close to being completely eliminated by poachers. It was concern over the survival of the bison that provided the impetus for the first attempts of wildlife management. In 1916 Congress established the National Park Service, a new bureau within the Department of the Interior, to address firmer management within all of the nation's national parks. The purpose of this organization was stated as follows:

> *The service thus established shall promote and regulate the use of the national parks...national parks, monuments and reservations...by such means and*

measures as conform to the fundamental purpose of said parks...which purpose is to conserve the scenery and the natural historic objects and the wild life therein and to provide for the enjoyment of the same in such manner and by such means as will leave them unimpaired for the enjoyment of future generations.

When management of Yellowstone came under the direction of Horace Albright in 1918, a team of park rangers were assembled and the first environmental education programs were established. These educational programs continue to be the keynote to preservation and management to this day.

While the wilderness within Yellowstone seems to be pretty well protected, advancing civilization and development around the perimeter could have a devastating impact on the Yellowstone ecosystem. Yellowstone's tremendous popularity and natural resources are also its most vexing problems. To the north and northwest nestled along the serene valleys created by the Madison, Gallation and Yellowstone rivers, alarming numbers of homes and ranches are emerging on what use to be pristine forests. Previously a huge buffer between Yellowstone and development, the Gallation National Forest to the north of the park has recently sold 165,000 acres to an Oregon firm. Environmentalists fear this land will be used for logging and development. It is currently inhabited by grizzly bear and elk.

While the forests may be "home" to a considerable amount of wildlife, it is also "home" to gold, copper, oil and platinum deposits. To the northeast lies a giant proposed gold mine site on the top of Henderson Mountain and to the west, timber cutting within the Targhee National Forest has created mile after mile of clear-cuts along the park's western border. What effects does this development have on the park itself? Water quality could be effected by the mining project, as it already is from older abandoned mines in the same area. Highways that are currently closed now to winter traffic would have to remain open year-round to allow access for mine employees to Cody, Wyoming.

Since the late 1980's, hunters and ranchers raising cattle along the Montana border of the park have been allowed to shoot bison that wander outside of the park's boundaries. Park bison could carry a disease called brucellosis, which has been known to cause cows to abort calves. At the time of this printing, the policy of shooting bison that leave the park is still under review.

Because bison, grizzly, elk and other wild animals are not aware that their only safety is within the confines of the park, they are subject to poaching of the worst degree when they leave its protective borders. Trophy hunters will pay up to $30,000 for a bighorn sheep.

25

Powdered elk antlers will sell for up to $40 an ounce to be used as aphrodisiacs in the Far East and bear claws are regarded as delicacies by some gourmets. It is clear that the wildlife itself stands in danger of elimination if the adjacent borders to the park do not act as a buffer for their protection.

In a time when we have so much destruction of our natural resources, overpopulation, pollution of air, soil and water, Yellowstone becomes even more valuable because of the pristine wilderness experience it promises to millions of visitors every year. We must therefore vehemently oppose anything which threatens to mutilate or destroy these perishable wonders ..."*the effect of a single evil upon the future of the park must be kept constantly in mind. The door once opened, though by ever so small a degree, cannot again be closed; but will sooner or later be thrown wide open. A privilege granted to one cannot be denied another...the only way to avoid these dangers is to keep the door entirely closed.*" Hiram Martin Chittenden, historian, 1895.

Greater Yellowstone: Today, it is healthy, wild, intricate and whole. Explore it, love it and protect it for it is a vibrant symbol of freedom, wonder, mystery and wildness like no other place on earth.

GEOLOGY

Volcanoes and Geysers

Turbulent pools of hot, boiling mud, barren landscapes, hot springs terraces, petrified forests, powerful steam vents and strange gaseous odors are rarities of nature found in only a very few places in the world. In no other place are they more abundant than in Yellowstone. These bizarre geologic formations are the result of volcanic eruptions that began nearly 2 million years ago. The last eruption occurred about 600,000 years ago and spewed out an incomprehensible 240 cubic tons of debris, collapsing what is now the park's central portion and forming a 28 by 47 mile caldera or basin. This cataclysmic event may have only lasted a few days, but enough volcanic debris and ash were spewed out to devastate the entire park region. Ashflows spewed at speeds of more than 100 miles per hour. Magma welled out, causing the underlying earth to collapse, creating a basin that in some areas was an unimaginable five or six thousand feet deep. By comparison, the eruption of Mt. St. Helens in 1980, ejected only one ten-thousandth of the volume of debris ejected at Yellowstone.

The magnetic heat that fueled those early eruptions still power the famous geysers of Yellowstone today. Geologists now believe that the source of this tremendous heat is due to an upwelling of magma, also known as magnetic plume, that lies just below the earth's

27

crust. In most areas of the world the earth's crust is between 15-30 miles thick. However, in Yellowstone this hot molten rock may be less than 2 miles deep; making it one of the hottest places on earth! Best estimates indicate the magma to be around 1700°F., measuring about 30 miles wide by 40 miles long. This magma heats the earth's surface, which in turn heats the water for the many geysers and hot springs. But heat and water are only two of the essentials needed to create geysers. The third element is "plumbing." Water, soaking into the ground from melting snow and precipitation, seeps deeply into the earth and channels its way through cracks in the rocks until it enters the vertical tubes of geysers. As water is heated by the magma, it becomes lighter in weight. This heated water rises above the cooler water that is flowing into the tubes and emerges in the form of geysers, boiling mud pots, fumaroles and hot springs. While steam and water are the most abundant elements that rise to the surface of geysers and hot springs, there is another even more obvious element you may have already noticed. Hydrogen sulfide, produced by geochemical reactions below the earth's surface, creates that pungent aroma you may refer to as that "rotten egg" smell.

While future volcanic eruptions are virtually certain, it's doubtful that any will occur within our lifetime.

YELLOWSTONE
Visitor Information
P.O. Box 168, Yellowstone National Park, Wyoming 82190, Telephone: (307) 344-7381

Area Attractions: ☐ Upper Loop ☐ Lower Loop ☐ Where to Find the Wildlife ☐ Lodging ☐ Camping ☐ Fishing ☐ Hiking ☐ Snowmobiling ☐ Boating

Entrances: From Cooke City, West Yellowstone and Gardiner, Montana; From Cody and Jackson Hole, Wyoming

Park Opens and Closes: Open to automobiles from approximately May 1 until the first big snow, usually around the beginning of November. Open to snowmobile and snowcoach traffic beginning mid-December until mid-March. The only road open year round is from Cooke City, Montana to the North Entrance.

Fees: Entrance, $10 per car or $4.00 for those entering by bike or on foot. This pass is good for 7 days and covers Teton National Park as well.

Parking: Provided throughout the park

Lodging: Old Faithful Inn, Old Faithful Snow Lodge, Old Faithful Lodge, Lake Yellowstone Hotel, Lake Lodge, Canyon Lodge, Grant Village, Roosevelt Lodge and the Mammoth Hot Springs Hotel. For detailed listing, see page 84.

Restaurants and Cafeterias: Old Faithful, Grant Village, Lake Yellowstone, Canyon Lodge, Roosevelt Lodge, Mammoth Hot Springs.

Visitor Centers: Grant Village, Old Faithful, Canyon, Fishing Bridge, Lake, Norris and Mammoth Hot Springs.

Medical Services:

Lake Hospital (Yellowstone Lake)	242-7241
Lake Clinic (Yellowstone Lake)	242-7241
Old Faithful Clinic	545-7325
Mammoth Clinic	344-7965
West Yellowstone Clinic	646-7668

Museums: Grant Village, Canyon, Fishing Bridge, Norris, Madison and Mammoth Hot Springs.

Gift Shops: Old Faithful, Lake, Canyon, Fishing Bridge, Grant Village, Roosevelt and Mammoth Hot Springs.

Service stations: Old Faithful, Grant Village, Fishing Bridge, Canyon, Tower and Mammoth

Hiking: On designated trails throughout park. Restrictions in some backcountry areas, check-in at ranger station. Various hikes are detailed throughout this book.

Backpacking: In designated campsites; permit required.

Bicycling: Permitted on public roads and prohibited on backcountry trails and boardwalks.

Horseback Riding: Mammoth, Canyon Lodge and Roosevelt Lodge. See page 145 for details.

Banking: 24-hour cash service is available in the Old Faithful lobby.

Campgrounds: 11 areas; 2 only for RVs. Fishing Bridge RV park has hookups and showers and can be reserved up to 8 weeks in advance. All others are on a first-come basis. See detailed listing on page 85.

Public showers: Old Faithful Lodge, Grant Village campground, Lake Lodge, Fishing Bridge RV park and Canyon Village campground.

Pets: Permitted on leashes. Not permitted in backcountry, public buildings, geyser areas or on trails.

Activities in Yellowstone: Cross-country skiing, snowmobiling, horseback riding, boating, fishing (fishing permit required) hiking, camping and bicycling.

LAKE YELLOWSTONE

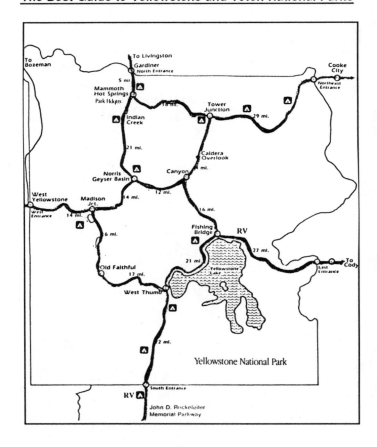

THE GRAND LOOP

34

Touring Yellowstone

ne of the most frequent complaints of visitors to Yellowstone is that they don't have enough time to see and experience all of the major attractions. There is simply so many areas to explore that, if your time is limited, you will have to make some concessions for a truly enjoyable vacation. I suggest you select a few attractions that interest you and really take your time to explore them thoroughly rather than speeding from one site to the next. Choose one or two nature trails to explore *leisurely* rather than *hurriedly* hiking a half dozen just to say you logged the miles.

With so much to do and see during your Yellowstone visit, I recommend at least 3 days to see the major attractions of the park. The park's road system is shaped like a figure eight and called the Grand Loop. The distance around the northern or Upper Loop is 70 miles and the distance around the southern or Lower Loop is 96 miles. While the maximum speed limit throughout the park is 45 miles an hour, actual driving time can vary dramatically. The roads through Yellowstone are narrow, steep in areas, winding and sometimes full of potholes. You may encounter wildly unpredictable weather conditions, especially in the spring, or an unyielding herd of tourists snapping pictures of an unyielding herd of bison. While it is possible to drive the Grand Loop in one

35

day, you will surely be cheating yourself of the more dazzling features of the park. Major attractions like Old Faithful and the magnificent Grand Canyon of Yellowstone can only be seen by parking your car and walking to the area. Try visiting major sites such as the Canyon or Old Faithful at dawn or dusk when the chance of encountering crowds is significantly reduced.

If you only heed one bit of advice, let it be this: Slow down. Stretch your legs on some of the nature trails. From an aerial viewpoint, the pavement, lakeshores and major attractions are swarming with strings of crowds. But the vast interior of the park, sometimes only slightly away from the road system, lies virtually untouched by man. The park has provided you with nearly 1,000 miles of backcountry trails to encourage this leisurely exploration. Take a stroll along one of the boardwalks on a bright moonlit night when the sights, sounds and smells are more intense. Another suggestion I might offer is to try to plan your visit in May or September when the crowds are gone. The wildlife is more abundant and relaxed, the spring and fall colors more vibrant and facilities are less crowded and expensive. These measures will all add to and enhance your Yellowstone visit.

There are five different ways to enter the park, all of which will lead you directly to the Grand Loop road that navigates the heart of Yellowstone. One of the most popular entrances is the south entrance from Jackson Hole. The south entrance road is located less than an hours drive north from Jackson via highway 89-191. Visitors should turn left at Moran Junction where you will enter Teton National Park and follow the shores of Jackson Lake until you reach the south entrance to Yellowstone. Once within the park's boundaries, you will begin your exploration of the lower loop of the figure eight road system. The route you take once you encounter your first junction will probably be based on your own personal interests, time limitations, etc..

The following list of attractions and sights are considered the highlights of Yellowstone you can expect to see traveling clockwise around each loop, using the major junctions in the park as reference points. We will begin our journey at the south entrance to Yellowstone.

Driving Distance from:	Miles
Billings to North Entrance	165
Billings to Northeast Entrance	127
Bozeman to North Entrance	79
Bozeman to West Entrance	90
Cody to East Entrance	53
Jackson to South Entrance	55

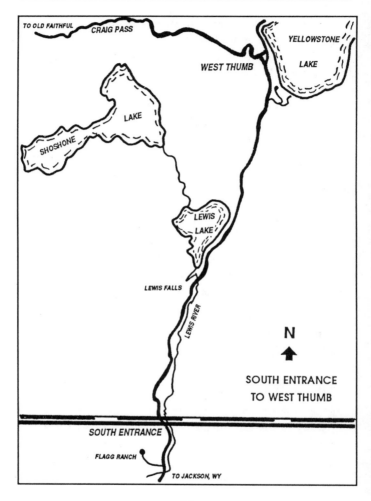

LOWER LOOP

South Entrance Road to West Thumb

☐ Lewis River Canyon

This deep 1.5 mile gorge plummets nearly 600 feet deep on either side into the tumbling Lewis River. This is a spectacular place to stop and witness the effects of the fires of 1988. In every direction as far as one can see, blackened lodgepole pines stand in quiet testament to the fierceness of the blaze.

☐ Lewis Falls

Lewis Falls is a wide, thundering fall with an abrupt drop of over 35 feet. The grassy meadow near the falls is a good area to spot the elusive moose.

☐ Lewis Lake

The third largest lake in Yellowstone, Lewis Lake offers an abundance of Mackinaw and brown trout. Approximately 4 miles north of the lake you'll cross the Continental divide at 7,988 feet.

☐ Shoshone Lake

Approximately 7.5 miles south of the Grant Village lies Shoshone Lake, Yellowstone's second largest lake and the largest inaccessible lake in North America. The area is approximately 12 square miles with the fascinating Shoshone Geyser Basin on the lake's west shore. The lake is approximately 5 miles from the main highway and is accessible only by trail or boat, making it a hiker's paradise. The trail is reached by an old road less than 1 mile north of the Lewis Lake campground.

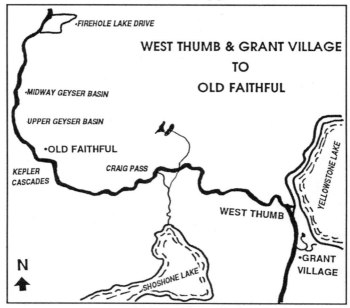

West Thumb and Grant Village to Old Faithful
Distance: 17 miles.

☐ Grant Village

One of the newest and more controversial developments to be built in Yellowstone, Grant Village was built in the 1980's to replace facilities at Fishing Bridge; closed in the early 1970's due to the high grizzly population. The development consists of a cluster of pink modernistic buildings including lodging, restaurants, gas station grocery store, campground and post office on the West Thumb of Yellowstone Lake. Unlike other facilities throughout the park, Grant Village lacks any of the natural and rustic charm one would expect to find in Yellowstone. **The Grant Village Visitor Center** is open from 8:30 to 5 mid-May through September and 8-8 mid-June through August and features exhibits on the fires of 1988.

☐ West Thumb

The steam plumes from West Thumb can be seen for miles, spewing from a thermal basin right on the shores of Yellowstone Lake. A short loop trail winds through the geyser basin past hot springs and geysers with names like Fishing Cone Geyser, Overhanging Geyser, Black Pool and Lakeside Spring. Visitors were once allowed to catch fish from Yellowstone Lake, then toss them into the geysers to simmer. This practice is no longer allowed.

☐ Lone Star Geyser

Approximately 15 miles from the West Thumb is a 2½ mile road that leads to the Lone Star Geyser. This 9 foot geyser cone erupts every three hours with sprays as high as 45 feet and lasts up to 30 minutes. This is also a popular and scenic place to ride your bike during the summer months.

☐ Kepler Cascades

Heading west from the West Thumb Junction, you will pass over the Continental Divide twice, once at 8,391 feet and again near Craig Pass at 8,262 feet. If not for the signs pinpointing the spots, you would hardly notice this gentle ascent and descent. Approximately 14 miles from the West Thumb, The Firehole River tumbles over Kepler Cascades. Pull off to the parking area on the left and walk the short boardwalk that juts out over the falls.

Old Faithful to Madison
Distance: 16 miles.

☐ Old Faithful and Upper Geyser Basin

Old Faithful is perhaps the most beloved and visited attraction in the park. No one leaves Yellowstone without first witnessing the geyser spray its 10,000 gallons of steaming hot water 100-180 feet into the air. Though Old Faithful is neither the tallest nor the most frequent geyser in the park, it has proved it be the most reliable and frequent **large** geyser, erupting every 75-90 minutes. The largest and most reliable of all the geysers in Yellowstone and the world, is the Grand. Shooting from a 10 foot high cone, the Grand erupts as high as 200 feet before resting for nearly six hours before its next eruption. With luck, and if you are willing to spend some time wandering the boardwalk around the basin, it is possible to enjoy a cornucopia of geyser activity in a single morning; Old

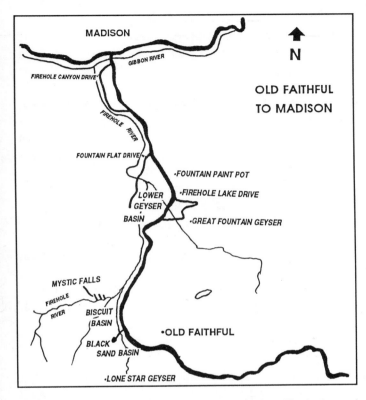

Faithful, of course, the Grand, Castle, Daisy, Firehole and Riverside. The boardwalk to the most popular circuit around the basin begins directly across from the inn. There are more than 40 different geysers here, emptying more than 68 tons of minerals daily into the Firehole River. Consider the size of the cavernous underground reservoir needed to hold that much water! Pick up a brochure for 25 cents that explains the different features of the geyser basin.

While it proves tempting for some folks to take a shortcut or wander off the boardwalks while visiting the extensive geyser basin around Old Faithful, this could be a serious mistake. The earth's crust is dangerously thin in some areas of the basin and visitors have been seriously scalded or killed after breaking through this thin layer. The remains of deer, bison and elk are frequently found in the thermal springs. Man has been as unsuccessful as animal when it comes to guessing the safety of these basins. Famous surveyor F.V. Hayden even broke through to seriously scald himself up to his knees. Even though bathing in thermal springs is prohibited, one young man thought he was jumping into a moderately warm pool, only to realize it measured over 178 degrees. He did not survive.

The National Park Service is constantly striving to protect its visitors by communicating hazards through the use of caution signs and warnings. It would be highly undesirable if guardrail and fences were constructed around such features. **Remember:** Every visitor to the park is inherently responsible for his own safety. The boardwalks are your only safety feature while

44

OLD FAITHFUL GEYSER

OLD FAITHFUL INN

in the thermal basin area. Be watchful of young children or anyone else in your party that is unable to understand the warning signs.

Once the geyser action is over, you will undoubtably want to check out the historic **Old Faithful Inn**. If you plan to stay at the inn during your Yellowstone visit, it is imperative that you book well in advance to assure availability, otherwise your chances of obtaining a room in mid-summer are practically nil.

The Old Faithful Inn is considered the largest log structure in the world. (While this claim has never been proven, no one as actually disputed it either.) It was designed by a Seattle architect named Robert C. Reamer and was constructed in 1903-1904. The main focus of Mr. Reamer's creative effort was on its impressive lobby. His talents have been appreciated by millions of visitors to Yellowstone ever since. Rustic in design, cavernous in size, its interior reaches upward 85 feet and is supported by huge gnarled logdepole burls which were cut within the park. In one corner is a massive fireplace containing over 500 tons of stone quarried from a site only 5 miles away. Above the fireplace hangs a giant clock designed by Reamer himself. Four spacious balconies above, provide a bird's-eye view of the dark warm interior.

Evenings can be quite special here. There is a fine restaurant located just off the lobby and after dinner drinks can be carried to the many nooks and crannies the old inn holds. Big rocking chairs creak in unison in front of a warm fire while piano music drifts over from a dark corner. There are many card tables and writing tables for the more industrious individuals or on warm summer nights you can sit on the upstairs balcony and watch Old Faithful erupting in the distance.

Tours of the Old Faithful Inn are given Thursday through Monday from 9:30 to 3:00 p.m.

The Old Faithful Visitor Center offers a large selection of books, maps and other helpful information. They are open daily from 9-4:30 and 8-8 during mid-summer.

❏ **Black Sand Basin, Biscuit Basin and Mystic Falls** Black Sand Basin is located about 1 mile from Old Faithful and Biscuit Basin is approximately another mile and a half further west. These basins are considered separate basins within the Upper Geyser Basin region. The most noteworthy geysers are located along the Firehole River. **Cliff Geyser**, located on Iron Creek, frequently spouts up to 30 feet in the air. Other interesting pools at Black Sand Basin are **Emerald Pool, Rainbow Pool, Handkerchief Pool** and **Sunset Lake**, all noted for their brightly colored algae and bacteria.

From the parking lot at Biscuit Basin, take the ½ mile nature walk across the Firehole River to noteworthy pools such as **Sapphire Pool, Black Opal Pool, Mustard Spring** and **Jewel Geyser**. From the far side of the boardwalk, a short 1 mile trail leads you along a forested and serene stretch of the Firehole River to the 70-foot **Mystic Falls**. For a longer hike, take the switchbacks to the top of the falls which connects with another trail that will lead you back down to Biscuit Basin. Total hiking distance is 3½ miles roundtrip.

☐ Midway Geyser Basin

At Midway Geyser Basin, you'll be treated to Yellowstone's largest hot spring; the **Grand Prismatic Springs**. The spring is also noted for its bright shades of reds and yellows created by algae and bacteria that grow in the pool despite the 170°F temperature. While springs are fairly numerous in the Midway Geyser Basin, you'll find less geyser activity here. **Excelsior Geyser** is the most famous of the geysers in Midway. In the 1880's this geyser was known to shoot huge explosions of steaming water over 380 feet into the air. One of these violent eruptions caused the plumbing for the geyser to burst, rendering it dormant for nearly a century.

☐ Lower Geyser Basin

The Lower Geyser Basin is an extension of the Midway Geyser Basin, the distinction being that it is topographically "lower" in the sense that it is located downstream from the Firehole River.

☐ Firehole Lake Drive

Once in the Lower Geyser Basin, you will notice a side road on the east side of the main road called Firehole

Lake Drive. This is a 3 mile one way loop road that will take you past Firehole Lake, the hottest lake in the park. To reach the lake itself you will need to take a short trail less than ½ mile in length. This trail will lead you past **Great Fountain** and **White Dome Geysers.** Great Fountain is a truly impressive geyser, erupting every 8-12 hours with blasts as high as 100 feet. White Dome Geyser is one of the oldest geysers in the park, evidenced by its huge 30-foot cone.

❏ Fountain Paint Pot

This is one of the most popular and finest thermal trails in the park. Numerous colorful mud springs can be found along the ½ mile Fountain Paint Pot Nature Trail. The mud gets its coloring from different sources, mainly the bacteria and algae it contains which creates alluring hues of orange and pink. Pick up a trail guide for 25 cents. It will explain the many features found along the nature trail.

❏ Fountain Flat Drive

Fountain Flat Drive forks from the main road just north of the Lower Geyser basin and passes through lush meadows along the Firehole River. This is an excellent place for watching bison and elk. This paved road ends after 3 miles, but you can reach the scenic 200-foot **Fairy Falls** area by hiking another 2½ miles beyond the barricade.

Firehole Canyon Drive

This southbound one way loop road begins just south of Madison and is about two miles in length. The road passes through the **Firehole Canyon** where steep rhyolite cliffs rise nearly 800 feet above the river. Firehole Falls is a beautiful fall that cascades over 40 feet. Next, you will pass the Firehole Cascades, another sight worth stopping to visit.

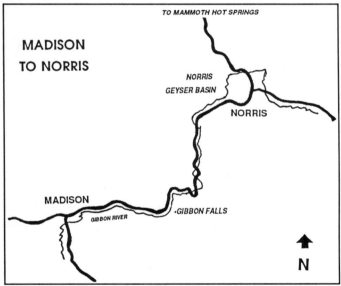

TO MAMMOTH HOT SPRINGS

MADISON
TO NORRIS

NORRIS
GEYSER BASIN

NORRIS

MADISON

GIBBON RIVER

·GIBBON FALLS

N

Madison to Norris
Distance: 14 miles.

☐ Madison Museum
The Madison Explorers Museum is located at Madison Junction and concentrates on the evolution of the park concept. It is open from dawn to dusk and is unstaffed.

☐ Gibbon Falls
Just north of Madison the road begins to parallel the Gibbon River for the next 13 miles. Approximately five miles from Madison you'll reach the scenic fall area. Gibbon Falls tumbles 84 feet over a wide ledge, then winds calmly through grassy meadows to join with the Firehole River and then eventually merge with the Madison River. Notice the burn area around the falls from the 1988 fires.

Norris to Canyon Village
Distance: 12 miles.

☐ Norris Geyser Basin
Norris Geyser Basin is ranked as the hottest and most thermal spot in the park and perhaps the hottest geyser basin in the world. Water temperature within the earth may register 706°F, the hottest temperature that water can be distinguished from gas. The paved road from the parking area will lead you to the **Norris Museum** which houses exhibits that explain the areas thermal features

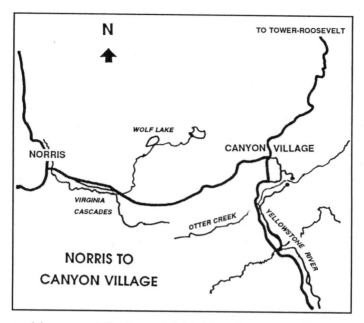

and is open daily from 9-4:30 May through September and 8-6 in mid-summer. Pick up a brochure for 25 cents that describes the special features at Norris. There are numerous and frequent eruptions at Norris, making it likely that you will see an eruption within any two hour period. Two separate trails wind through the geyser basins, each making a loop. They are both worth taking.

☐ Virginia Cascade

The road from Norris to Canyon cuts across the center of the park and passes through one of the most fire devastated areas of Yellowstone. However, not all of the damage was caused by the fires of 1988. In 1984, a severe windstorm swept through this region, uprooting miles of lodgepole forests. The dried trees went up in an inferno when the '88 fires raged through the area. Less than 4 miles east of Norris you'll approach Virginia Cascades Road. This is a one way loop road that will follow 2.5 miles along the rushing Gibbon River and allow you a view of the 60 foot tall Virginia Cascades. The loop then leads you back onto the main highway. Once back on the highway, you'll be in a good area for spotting elk and bison.

Canyon Village to Lake
Distance: 16 miles.

☐ Grand Canyon of the Yellowstone

Though the geysers are playful, the lakes cool and serene, the massive snowcapped mountains majestic, nothing quite prepares you for the immense, powerful beauty of the Grand Canyon of the Yellowstone. Here

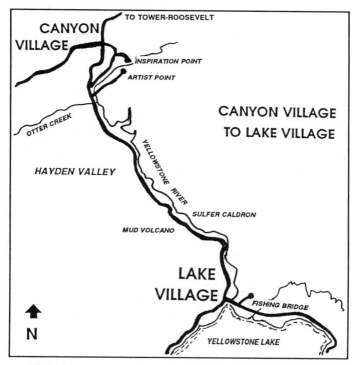

CANYON VILLAGE

TO TOWER-ROOSEVELT

INSPIRATION POINT

ARTIST POINT

OTTER CREEK

CANYON VILLAGE
TO LAKE VILLAGE

HAYDEN VALLEY

YELLOWSTONE RIVER

SULFER CALDRON

MUD VOLCANO

LAKE VILLAGE

FISHING BRIDGE

N

YELLOWSTONE LAKE

you'll find a great gash slashed through the earth where waters roar, rivers foam and churn and falls tumble and sparkle in the brilliance of the sun. This is where the river, the lake and the park itself received its namesake: from the yellow vertical walls of this magnificent gorge.

The canyon is more than 20 miles long and 4,000 feet across. Colorful, ragged cliffs drop as much as 1,200 feet into the winding river below. The river hurtles violently over two great falls: first the Upper Falls, dropping more than 110 feet and then plunging more than 300 feet over the famous Lower Falls. Here, the thunderous roar can be heard for miles along the rim.

The predominantly yellow walls of the canyon are formed of rhyolite. This rhyolite softened over time due to hot gasses and water, making it very susceptible to erosion. In the past half million years, massive glaciers blocked water upstream forming huge glacial lakes near the head of the canyon. Repeatedly, they have overflowed and ripped through the softened rhyolite walls to form the canyon you see today. Near the rim at Inspiration Point, you will find a large boulder left here more than 15,000 years ago from a receding glacier. It came from an area more than 15 miles away.

There are several scenic overlooks offering different views of the canyon and roads around each of the rims with frequent turn-outs. You'll also find many marked trails around each of the rims, some affording you dramatic close-up vistas of the falls.

THE GRAND CANYON OF THE YELLOWSTONE

☐ Canyon Village

Located on the North Rim, Canyon Village offers gift shops, groceries, restaurants, a post office and a gas station. You'll also find cabins and a campground here. Because this is grizzly country, only hard sided RV's are allowed.

☐ Canyon Visitor Center

Try to stop at the Canyon Visitor Center before you begin your exploration of the canyon. The exhibits here provide information about the formation and history of the canyon. While here, pick up a map of the canyon area. It will provide you with descriptions of the many overlooks and scenic trails along the north and south rims. Hours are from 9-5, May through September.

☐ North Rim

The northernmost view is from Inspiration Point, providing you with a full perspective of the falls and canyon. Here you first realize the shear depth and magnitude of the canyon. The canyon bottom is nearly 1,000 feet below you. Near the rim at Inspiration Point, you'll notice the large boulder discussed earlier that was deposited here by retreating glaciers more than 15,000 years ago. Near this boulder is the **Seven Mile Hole Trail**. It is actually only 5 miles long and it offers magnificent views of the canyon. The trail follows a series of switchbacks down to the river below. This is a favorite destination for fishing or for those who want to enjoy the river without the crowds. The hike back up is a little more grueling. There is a saying about hiking down into the canyon: "3 miles down, 35 miles back up..." The next stop, once you rejoin the one-way road, is to the overlooks of **Grandview** and **Lookout Point**. From Grandview, you'll view the falls unobstructed, but from a distance. Lookout Point provides a classic perspective of the Lower Falls. From Lookout Point, a ½ mile trail descends several hundred feet into the canyon to **Red Rock Point**, providing you closer inspection of the falls. Back on the main highway, the next turn-off will take you to the **Brink of the Upper Falls**. Standing at the brink of the Upper Falls offers you the opportunity to ponder the astounding force of 64 thousand gallons of water per second, rushing over the falls to the river below.

❑ South Rim

For sheer drama, the south rim overlooks are unmatched. Cross the Yellowstone River at the Chittenden Bridge and continue ½ mile and park in Uncle Tom's parking area. There are two trails here. One is a short trail that takes you to overlooks of the Upper Falls and Crystal Falls. For the more ambitious hiker, **Uncle Tom's Trail** is an impressive way to gain a close-up view of the Lower Falls. You'll begin this trail by taking a series of descending switchbacks, then when the descent becomes too steep the trail turns into a series of metal steps; 328

in all. This trail was named after "Uncle" Tom Richardson, an enterprising individual, who led paying tourists down a series of ropes and wooden ladders to the base of the falls. His park permit was revoked in 1903 and today, the trip down is free. A mile after Uncle Tom's parking area, is the parking area for **Artist Point**. This is the dramatic viewpoint from which wilderness artist Thomas Moran was inspired to paint his famous watercolors.

❑ Hayden Valley

The 16 mile road from Canyon to Lake Junction passes through the beautiful and serene Hayden Valley, named after Dr. Ferdinand V. Hayden, a geologist who surveyed and mapped Yellowstone in 1871.

Hayden Valley was once the floor of a huge glacial lake that receded leaving behind rich sediments of soil. While this soil promotes little tree growth, it does allow an abundance of shrubs, grasses and sage to flourish, providing a premier grazing area for a variety of wildlife. This is a prime viewing area for moose, bison and an occasional grizzly. Dozens of streams and rivulets branch off the Yellowstone River and flow through the valley creating lush marshy areas for trumpeter swans, geese, white pelicans and many varieties of ducks.

❑ Sulfur Caldron

Sulfur Caldron is located on the east side of the road ½ mile after leaving the southern end of Hayden Valley. This is one of the most acidic springs in the park (containing a pH of approximately 1.2-the same as battery acid) and the bright yellow coloring is an indication of its heavy concentration of hydrogen sulfide.

☐ Mud Volcano

The Mud Volcano area is a sure indication that this is a uniquely strange part of the world. This is perhaps one of the more interesting thermal basins in Yellowstone because of the ominous violent, churning and hissing you'll witness when investigating areas with names like Dragon's Mouth, Cooking Hillside, Mud Volcano and Black Dragon's Caldron. While the water in this area doesn't actually reach boiling point at only 180 degrees, the boiling action you see is actually caused by carbon dioxide and other gasses rising to the pool's surface. Pick up one of the pamphlets that explain this area. It costs 25 cents and provides you with a map and a detailed description of the features around the basin. If time permits, a moonlit night visit to this area can conjure up some exciting images of what the world could have been like in its primordial phase, millions of years ago.

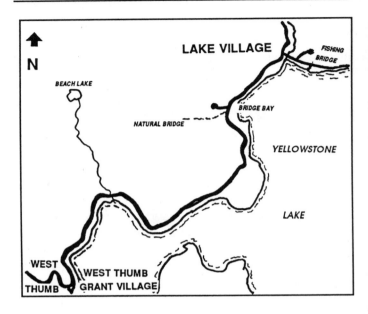

Lake Junction to West Thumb
Distance: 21 miles

☐ Fishing Bridge

The famous Fishing Bridge was built in 1937 and spans the Yellowstone River, the one outlet of Yellowstone Lake. Though it was once a favorite fishing spot among anglers who came for the abundance of cutthroat trout, fishing has been prohibited here since 1973 because of the high level of grizzly activity. Considered a very important habitat area for the grizzly, unnecessary conflicts between fishermen and bears has caused the destruction of more than 16 of these majestic animals. It has now become a favorite fishing ground to the white pelicans who feed on the rich supply of native cutthroat trout.

Because of the high incidence of bear activity, only hard sided RV's are allowed to camp at Fishing Bridge.

The **Fishing Bridge Visitor's Center** is open daily from 8:30 to 5 and features the birds of Yellowstone.

☐ Lake Yellowstone Hotel

The Lake Yellowstone Hotel is the oldest and by far the most elegant hotel in Yellowstone. It was built in 1889-1891 and designed by the same architect that designed the Old Faithful Inn; Robert Reamer. The large pale yellow building has tall white columns gracing its front, which faces the crystal-clear waters of Yellowstone Lake. Once inside, sit with a cool beverage in the hotel's lobby and enjoy the live piano music, which is played most afternoons and evenings. You'll be treated to arresting views of the lake and the Absaroka Mountain Range in the distance. The hotel offers fine dining, cafeteria dining, gift shops and a beauty shop.

Other facilities in Lake Village include rustic cabin lodging at **Lake Lodge**, a Hamilton store, hospital, gas station and post office.

☐ Yellowstone Lake

Yellowstone Lake is a stunning sight to behold. Awesome in its sheer size and beauty, it stretches 20 miles long, 14 miles wide and offers 110 miles of pristine shoreline. It is 320 feet at its deepest spot. Its immense dimensions were formed by the melting and runoff of ancient glaciers nearly 12,000 years ago. At that time, the lake was more than double the size that it is today.

While the water is much too cold for swimming, it is excellent for boating and canoeing. It is advisable to know the weather conditions predicted for the day. Small boats have been known to capsize in the rolling waves when the weather turns nasty.

☐ Bridge Bay

Bridge Bay consists of a campground, marina, marina store and ranger station. Boat rentals are available.

☐ Natural Bridge

Directly south of Bridge Bay you will find a turn-off to Natural Bridge, an arch of stone nearly 60 feet in height, carved naturally from the waters of Bridge Creek.

YELLOWSTONE LAKE

65

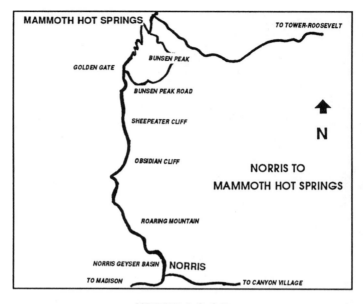

UPPER LOOP

Norris to Mammoth Hot Springs
Distance: 21 miles.

⬛ **Norris Geyser Basin: See page 52.**

⬛ **Roaring Mountain**

Approximately 4½ miles from Norris is Roaring Mountain, a high, steaming hill near the roadside. Roaring Mountain earned its name in the early 1900's when fumaroles became violently active, creating huge and audible roars from the mountainside. It is considerably more tame today.

☐ Obsidian Cliff

Obsidian Cliff, also called Glass Mountain, consists of black lustrous rocks that formed when lava cooled very quickly nearly 150,000 years ago. Because of its hard fine texture, these cliffs proved valuable to early Indians for the making of knives and projectile points.

☐ Sheepeater Cliffs

From the name of the only known inhabitants of Yellowstone, the Sheepeater Indians. The cliffs are columns of basalt; volcanic rock formed during cooling.

☐ Bunsen Peak Road

This 6 mile one-way loop road begins just south of Golden Gate Road. This is a dirt road and some spots are very rough making it off-limits to RV's and trailers. The road circles Bunsen Peak, an 8,565-foot volcanic cone named after Robert F. Bunsen. Bunsen was the first individual to explain the dynamics of geysers action and invented the Bunsen burner.

☐ Golden Gate Canyon

Directly after the Bunsen Peak Road is the Golden Gate loop road. This is a 7 mile, one-way road that winds through the Golden Gate Canyon and alongside Glen Creek. The Golden Gate Canyon received its name because of the vivid yellow lichen that grows on its cliffs.

At the head of the canyon is **Rustic Falls**, a pretty waterfall of Glen Creek.

☐ Hoodoos

If you stay on the main road instead of taking the Bunsen Peak Road or Golden Gate, you will find a short loop road just south of Mammoth that will take you to the Hoodoos. These enormous travertine rock formations were created thousands of years ago by hot springs. They have tipped from their original horizontal positions creating a delightful jumble of boulders pointing in all directions.

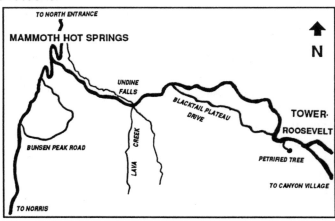

Mammoth Hot Springs to Tower-Roosevelt
Distance: 18 miles.

☐ Mammoth Hot Springs

Mammoth Hot Springs lies close to the northern border of Yellowstone and is the administrative and business headquarters of the park. The gateway city of Gardiner, Montana is located just to the north and is open to automobiles year-round, making the northern entrance to Yellowstone another popular starting point for visitors.

Mammoth is the only region within the park where such extensive development was allowed to exist. Many of the buildings you see here today were part of old Fort Yellowstone. The park was patrolled by soldiers until 1916 and the fort was the headquarters of the officers assigned to the management of Yellowstone. Today, the buildings are occupied by park officials, a ranger station, museum, visitors center, etc..

Mammoth Hot Springs gushes and spews more than 700,000 gallons of hot mineral water every 24 hours, adding literally tons of travertine to the already huge multi-hued terraces daily. The source of its water is from rain and heavy snows. As the precipitation seeps into the earth it encounters volcanic magma. This magma is extremely high in carbon dioxide and when mixed with the water, becomes carbonic acid. This highly acidic water passes through and dissolves the area's sedimentary limestone as it rises its way to the surface at Mammoth. As the water flows over the travertine terraces, it deposits the limestone sediment that it has carried up from within the earth. These additional limestone deposits create an astounding growth on the steps at a rate of up to eight inches a year!

The Mammoth Hot Springs area encompasses a huge hillside and contains dozens of springs of all shapes and sizes. Most of these springs can be reached by the boardwalk around the Lower Terrace or by the 1.5 mile Upper Terrace Drive. You can walk from the Lower Terrace to the Upper Terrace by taking the steps that connects the two. Pick up a 25 cent brochure for a complete descriptions of the springs. Three of the most noteworthy springs here are **Minerva Terrace, Jupiter Terrace** and **Canary Spring**. Near the Lower Terrace parking area, look for the **Liberty Cap**. This is a 35 foot mass of travertine named by the Hayden Survey for its resemblance to the peaked caps worn during the French Revolution. On the Upper Terrace is Poison Spring, a sinkhole with a high carbon dioxide content. The gasses here prove poisonous to the many birds that come to sip the deadly brew. In one season from May through November, a total of 236 birds were found dead around the small pool. Cross the road to visit **Opal Terrace**, the most active of all the springs here.

MAMMOTH HOT SPRINGS

☐ Albright Visitor Center

The visitor center is spread out over two floors and features exhibits, films and slideshows concerning history and wildlife within the park. You'll find a great selection of books, maps and photographs and an information desk with plenty of free information and brochures to Yellowstone's interior. Also featured here are over 20 watercolors of painter Thomas Moran and some of the famous photographs taken by William H. Jackson during the Hayden Survey.

The center is open year-round, 8:30-5:00 with extended hours during mid-summer.

☐ Mammoth Hot Springs Hotel

The original Mammoth Hotel was once described by writer Rudyard Kipling as "a huge yellow barn". He also noted how the ground around the hotel "rings hollow like kerosene tin" and predicted that "the Mammoth Hotel, guests and all, will sink into the caverns below and be turned into stalactite!" That was in 1889. The Mammoth Hot Springs Hotel you see today was constructed in 1937 and seems to be holding its own quite well. Step inside and admire the huge wooden map of the United States. Other facilities at Mammoth include a gas station, Hamilton Store, post office, restaurants and horseback riding facilities. You will find the Mammoth Campground a short distance down the road.

☐ Undine Falls

Four miles from Mammoth is beautiful Undine Falls, a double waterfall spilling over 60 feet down and over a series of steps. A half a mile further is **Wraith Falls,** nestled in a forested glade of pine, spruce and fir.

☐ Blacktail Plateau Drive

This is a rough 7 mile dirt road located approximately 9 miles east of Mammoth. The road partially parallels the old Bannock Trail, a trail used in the 1830's till the 1890's by the Bannock Indians on their way to hunting grounds in search of bison. You can still see the deep travois furrows in the grassy slopes, though it has remained unused for the past 100 years.

☐ Petrified tree

Approximately ½ mile after Blacktail Plateau Drive re-enters the main highway, you'll see a turn-off that will lead you to the petrified tree. This fifty million year old redwood tree stands some 20 feet high behind a heavy iron fence. This barrier is to prevent it from being carried off chip by chip as was the fate of a similar tree located in the same area.

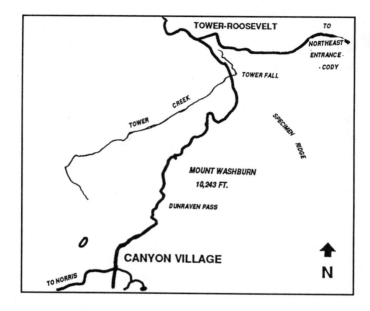

Tower-Roosevelt to Canyon Village
Distance: 31 miles.

☐ Roosevelt Lodge

Popular legend has it that during President Theodore Roosevelts' stay in Yellowstone in 1903, he camped at the very sight of the current Roosevelt Lodge. However, it is now known that was a complete fabrication generated by Howard Hayes to publicize his Roosevelt Lodge. While the lodge was named by Hayes in 1920 in the president's honor, the presidents camp was actually a few miles south of the site.

The main lodge offers a family style restaurant (popular for the barbecued ribs), 2 large fireplaces and a long porch with plenty of rocking chairs. Other facilities here include a gift shop and horseback riding facilities.

❑ Calcite Springs

Approximately 2 miles south of Tower-Roosevelt junction is an overlook to Calcite Springs. Take the short trail for an impressive view to the bottom of the canyon. On the canyon floor is Calcite Springs. The river lies 500 feet below and flows through the narrowest section of any of the four gorges of the Yellowstone River.

❑ Overhanging Cliff

Located 1½ miles south of Calcite Springs is Overhanging Cliff, flanking the road for some 50 yards with huge columns of basalt

❑ Tower Fall

Approximately 2.5 miles south of the Tower-Roosevelt junction is the parking area for Tower Fall. Follow the short path that leads to the observation platform near the fall. One of the prettiest falls in the park, Tower Fall drops 132 feet to the deep blue waters of the Yellowstone River below. Black, miniature towers of volcanic rock edge the brink of the fall, which is how the fall received its name. For more than a century a prominent feature of the fall was a huge boulder that perched precariously at the brink of the falls. This boulder led to countless speculations and bets between early explorers about how long it would be before nature sent it over the edge. They would be surprised to learn that it would not be until 1986 that the boulder finally succumbed to the force of water and nature. To the right of the overlook there is a footpath that switchbacks down to the base of the falls. From this vantage point the fall is even more beautiful. For a detailed description of the hiking trails in this area, see page 136.

☐ Mount Washburn

Heading south from Tower Fall, is the 10,243-foot mountain, named Mt. Washburn. Named after the surveyor of the Washburn Expedition in 1870, Washburn climbed the summit and wrote of it:

"I saw the canyon and the lake. There are unmistakable columns of steam in the distance. This is a glorious region."

Because of its central location within the park, the summit of Mt. Washburn provides one of the most impressive overviews of the Yellowstone region. For a detailed description of the hike to the summit of Mt.

Washburn, see the hiking section of this guide on page 134.

☐ Dunraven Pass

Approximately 5 miles south of Mt. Washburn is Dunraven Pass: elevation 8,850 feet. This section of road is the highest point in the park reached by a public road. It is named for the Earl of Dunraven, who visited the park in 1874 and promoted Yellowstone to wealthy European travelers through his book titled "*The Great Divide*."

THE FIRES OF '88

Fires are a fact of life in the forest and the fires of 1988 changed Yellowstone in an incredibly dramatic way. This wilderness has not seen such uncontrolled fury since 1910, when fires swept across Idaho, Montana and the Greater Yellowstone area, consuming more than 5 million acres.

The summer months of 1988 were the driest in Yellowstone's 112 years of recorded weather conditions. By early summer, the extremely dry conditions had already caused more than 20 lightening-caused fires. By mid-July, the park prudently suspended its "let-burn" policy and began to battle the blazes in earnest. More than 25,000 fire-fighting personnel were brought in, (at a cost of more than $120 million) but it made little difference. Aided by unusually strong wind gusts of up to 70 mph, fire engulfed, in one single day (September 7), more than 100,000 acres and 20 buildings around Old Faithful. By the time the fires were subdued (with the help of an early snow), more than 1.6 million acres were burned; an area larger than the state of Delaware.

While the controversy surrounding the "let-burn" policy continues to rage on 5 years later, Yellowstone is in a state of rebirth. Everywhere you look in Yellowstone, there are signs of recovery. Wildflowers blaze in Antelope Valley, grasses grow waist-deep in Blacktail Deer Plateau and scarlet fireweed has sprouted at Lupine Creek.

While it may be disappointing to some visitors to witness so much of Yellowstone charred by the fires (nearly 35% of the park), few scientists would disagree that it is possible or even desirable to control every fire in Yellowstone. Fire, in some instances, is an absolute necessity, especially for the continued germination of some species of trees.

Take the time to walk through some of the burn areas, especially the self-guided "Children's Fire Trail" near Mammoth.

Where to Find the Wildlife

O ne of the most delightful experiences of your Yellowstone visit will be the encountering of wildlife. (Please remember to observe without approaching. Every animal is tolerant to a certain degree, then may feel threatened enough to charge if approached any further.) As suggested earlier in this book, to catch wildlife in its most abundant and relaxed state, plan your visit to the park in May or September when the crowds have not yet arrived and the park is quiet. Snow forces herds into lower elevations making winter an excellent time to visit the park. While the roads are closed to automobile traffic during November to April, you can visit the park either by snowcoach, cross-country skiing or snowmobile. No matter what time of the year, you can witness, in most cases, a wide variety of wildlife (elk, deer, bison and coyote) alongside the park's roadway, especially around dusk. The most common herd animal in the park is the **elk**, with a summer population of around 20,000. During summer, most elk migrate to higher elevations, but enough linger around to assure plenty of opportunity for viewing. Look for elk especially between Mammoth and Old Faithful, from Yellowstone Lake to the east entrance and along the Madison River. In the winter, most elk move north to the Yellowstone River Valley or south into Jackson Hole.

Moose, the largest animal in the deer family, are usually solitary in nature or move in bands of two to four. They are equal to the horse in size, stand five to six feet at the shoulder and are nearly half a ton in weight. They are also one of the more unpredictable and dangerous animals in the forest you are likely to encounter. Your most promising areas to view moose are along the Lewis River, in Hayden and Lamar Valleys, between Fishing Bridge and the east entrance and in Swan Lake Flat. They feed, nearly submerged at times, on riverbottoms, coming up after 30-40 seconds with snoutfulls of soggy vegetation or "moose-muck".

There are few sights that will elicit more fear or excitement than a **grizzly** sow bear with her cubs. The fact that this majestic creature still roams these parts is testament to the tremendous conservation efforts of groups such as the Greater Yellowstone Coalition

Organization, who have worked to protect and expand the habitat for bears. Yellowstone is one of the last places in the lower 48 states where these animals have survived. Yet the numbers still spell potential disaster for the species. There are only 1,000 grizzlies left in the entire lower 48 states; that's only 1% of their estimated population of over 100,000 in the 1800's. Without more protected habitat areas such as Yellowstone, the long-term survival of the grizzly is significantly threatened.

While bear encounters are rare because of the wary nature of the species, there is nothing more dangerous or potentially injurious than a collision course with man and grizzly. The first recorded grizzly attack in the park was in 1907. A visitor to the park chased a young cub up a tree and began to prod it with an umbrella for the amusement of himself and onlookers. This antic proved to be fatal to the surprised "prankster" when the enraged mother bear showed up and retaliated with her own beastly "prodding". Beginning in 1919, feeding shows began in the park for the "entertainment" of the visitors. Park rangers supplied garbage to various feeding stations in the park, giving evening talks about the wild, while up to 50 bears gathered 'round for their evening buffet. However, it proved dangerous to associate the presence of humans with food and the practice was stopped in 1941. Unfortunately, the following years brought more than 50 deaths to grizzlies because

81

of their unhealthy attraction to garbage sights and humans.

Today there are more than 200 grizzlies in Yellowstone and approximately 500 black bear. (Roughly one fifth of the park is closed at various times in the interest of the grizzly.) Because of these low numbers, grizzlies were listed in 1975 as a threatened species in the lower 48 states. While progress has been made to protect the species, grizzly habitat continues to shrink due to human development.

The more likely areas to spot grizzly or **black bears** in Yellowstone, bearing in mind you want to maintain a considerable distance, is Pelican Valley and around the shores of Yellowstone Lake. Occasional sightings have also been observed in Hayden Valley.

The **bison**, a mammal exclusive to North America, was hunted nearly to extinction by the time Yellowstone became a national park. In 1902, only 25 remained. The 2,500 that populate the park today are only a remanent of the millions that once roamed this region. As the herd dwindled to alarmingly small numbers, plains bison were brought in from private ranches in Texas and Montana to breed with the original mountain bison; meaning the animals today are genetically different from their original ancestors. A subject of controversy is the policy of private ranchers being permitted to shoot bison once they leave the protection of the park. Bison carry a disease called brucellosis, which causes cows to abort calves. During the winter of 1988-89, more than five hundred bison were shot as they left the park's boundaries in search of food. This policy is currently under review.

Bison head for high country in summer, but many numbers can still be seen along the northeast shore of Yellowstone Lake, Hayden Valley and along the Firehole and Lamar Rivers.

Mule deer can be found anywhere throughout Yellowstone, especially at dusk and early in the day. **Antelope** can be spotted year round in the Lamar Valley and in the Gardiner area.

The **coyote**, a once persecuted animal in Yellowstone, is now understood to play a major role in the balance of nature within Yellowstone. They are fully protected within the park, but by no means considered rare. Coyotes subsist mainly on small rodents such as mice, snowshoe hare and pocket gophers. While a small portion of the coyotes diet does consist of deer or other large game, it is mostly those that have died from other causes, such as malnutrition, disease or crippling.

While larger animals seem to attract the most attention in Yellowstone, the smaller wildlife is equally interesting. The park's abundant birdlife population includes bald eagles, golden eagles, trumpeter swans, great blue herons, sandhill cranes, ravens, Canadian Geese and white pelicans.

There are at least 16 different species of fish in Yellowstone, including the largest population of native **cutthroat trout** in the world. Fishing regulations are stringent, for the benefit of the fish, and anglers are urged to release fish after they are caught.

LODGING IN YELLOWSTONE

The following list of accommodations in the park are based on a 1-2 person rate during the high season. For more specific rate information, call **TWR Services** at 307-344-7311. They're the official concessionaire for lodging in Yellowstone.

LOCATION	HOTEL ROOMS	CABINS
Canyon Lodge Cabins		$46-62
Grant Village	$48-49	
Lake Lodge Cabins		$40-62
Lake Yellowstone Hotel and Cabins	$60-95	$45
Mammoth Hot Springs Hotel and Cabins	$35-50	$21-48
Old Faithful Inn	$32-65	
Old Faithful Snow Lodge and Cabins	$35	$45-62
Roosevelt Lodge Cabins		$20-48

CAMPING

There are eleven campsites available in Yellowstone. With the exception of *Bridge Bay, all campsites are available on a first-come, first-serve basis. All camping is limited to a 14 day stay between July 1, and Labor Day, and to 30 days the remainder of the year. Check-out times for all facilities is 10:00 a.m.. Because these sights fill up early during the summer season, it is advisable to obtain your campsite as early in the day as possible.

CAMPGROUND	DUMP STATION	SITES	FEE	TOILET
Bridge Bay	Yes	420	$10.00	Flush
Canyon	Yes	280	8.00	Flush
Grant Village	Yes	414	8.00	Flush
Madison	Yes	292	8.00	Flush
Mammoth	No	85	8.00	Flush
Norris	No	116	8.00	Flush
Indian Creek	No	75	6.00	Pit
Lewis Lake	No	85	6.00	Pit
Pebble Creek	No	36	6.00	Pit
Slough Creek	No	29	6.00	Pit
Tower Fall	No	32	6.00	Pit

*Bridge Bay campsites can be reserved by calling Mistix Reservations at (800) 365-2267.

OTHER RECREATION IN YELLOWSTONE

During the summer and winter months there are many recreational activities available in Yellowstone. These activities include snowmobiling, boating and canoeing, horseback riding and bicycling. A description of these activities can be found under each individual heading, beginning on page 123 of this guide.

"Within this space
the Creator
must have intended
to bring man
in humility
to his knees."

Margaret E. Murie

GRAND TETON
NATIONAL PARK

INTRODUCTION

T he Shoshone Indians called them the Teewinot (many Peaks) and the french called them Le' Trois Teton (the three breasts). Everyone calls them beautiful. The most imposing sight in Grand Teton National Park is, of course, the Grand Teton Range rising 12,000 feet from the valley floor. The dominating peak is the Grand Teton; rising in a jagged cathedral spiral to a height of 13,770 feet. As far as mountains go, they are neither the longest range along the Rockies nor the tallest. They are, however, the grandest and most inspiring, with their pinnacled, snow-capped peaks and deeply chiseled canyons. Though this magnificent range has caught the awed praises of countless visitors who invariable find themselves uttering words such as, "magnificent," "absolutely beautiful," and "breathtaking," it is only a slice of what the park is all about.

The stunning 50-mile long valley (known as Jackson Hole) that encompasses Grand Teton National Park offers some of the most stunning scenery to be found anywhere in the Rockies. During the summer season, visitors come to float the Snake River, hike the numerous mountain trails, fish the many lakes and streams and camp under the shadow of the Tetons. Spring and autumn are perhaps the most intense and beautiful months to arrive in the valley. The colors are more vibrant, the wildlife more plentiful, accommodations readily available and the pace less hurried. With winter comes a sense of peacefulness and purity unlike any other time in the valley. Around November, snow begins to cover the valley and the Tetons become a Mecca for winter recreation. In addition to world class skiing, this is the time for sleigh rides, snowmobiling, cross-country skiing or simply soaking in a hot thermal spring while feathery light snow falls gently around you. Whatever the season, you'll experience some of the best in rocky mountain scenery and recreation that any place has to offer.

The park harbors dozens of sparkling lakes and streams and an abundance of wildlife inhabiting emerald green forests and rugged canyons. Dozens of canyon trails beckon exploration with enticing names like Avalanche Canyon, Cascade Canyon and Death Canyon. More than 200 miles of trails offer a variety of backcountry experiences. The adventurous can saddle-up on horseback for a ride through craggy canyons on cliff-hugging trails. For a more sedate experience, take a stroll along a shimmering glacial lake or picnic in a sunny, grassy meadow. If the only thing permitted here was quite observation of the beauty that surrounds you, Grand Teton National Park would still remain high on my list of "most desirable" places in the world to visit. However, activities abound here. It is a haven for skiing, boating, fishing, snowmobiling and camping.

GEOLOGY

The Tetons are a distinctive range among the Rockies. For starters, they are our youngest mountains, only 10 million years old compared to an age of about 60 million years of nearby ranges. They are not your usual type of mountain range in that there are no foothills *whatsoever* nor is there a gradual slope from the base to the peaks. They rise abruptly from the valley floor and are tilted to the west, with their peaks pointing east. These mountains are clearly the most asymmetrical mountains on the planet.

The formation of these unusual mountains began some nine million years ago when deep pressure within the earth caused a series of breaks, called **faults**, in the earth's crust. The most spectacular fault was the Teton Fault, some 40 miles long and just west of what is now Jackson Hole.

The Tetons were formed when a 12 mile wide block of earth to the west of the fault began to rise steadily upward. Jackson Hole was formed when the eastern block abruptly dropped away.

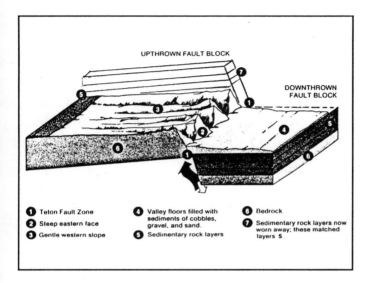

UPTHROWN FAULT BLOCK

DOWNTHROWN FAULT BLOCK

❶ Teton Fault Zone	❹ Valley floors filled with sediments of cobbles, gravel, and sand.	❻ Bedrock
❷ Steep eastern face		❼ Sedimentary rock layers now worn away; these matched layers 5
❸ Gentle western slope	❺ Sedimentary rock layers	

At first, the Tetons had a completely different look than the range you see before you. Its peaks were not as pointed or defined as they are today. This happened later when erosion began to strip away the overlying sediments. In some areas, this sediment was stripped away entirely, exposing ancient crystalline rock jutting up to become the mountain's lofty ragged peaks.

After the range had reached its full height, another important event began that would further carve and shape the range as you see it today; the formation of glaciers. Glaciers form when more snow falls in winter than can melt away by summer, creating huge snowfields. As the weight of this accumulated snow increases, it eventually compresses and turns to ice. Gravity eventually begins to slowly pull this ice downhill. As the glaciers slowly swept down the mountain range, they began to carve and shape steep canyons walls. (Cascade Canyon is a spectacular example of glacial carving.) These rivers of slowly moving ice picked up tons of debris along the way and carried it down to the valley. After the glaciers melted, large piles of glacial debris were left along the glacier's rim, called **moraines**. These moraines are responsible for creating natural dams that formed Jenny, Leigh, Bradley, Taggart, and Phelps lakes.

HISTORY

ore than 10,000 years ago, a small tribe began a tenuous journey across the steep mountain passes into Jackson Hole. They were on foot, no doubt, and probably in search of wild game. They would not be disappointed. Summers in this valley were a veritable paradise. The area was rich in buffalo, deer, elk, and pronghorn sheep. An abundance of flora and fauna could be collected from the valley floor to constitute the balance of their diets. By late summer these early people would be off in search of more hospitable hunting territories. Winters in this valley were much too brutal and wildlife too scarce to be considered as a permanent home.

EARLY TRAPPERS AND EXPLORERS

I n the 1700's, the Spanish would introduce the horse to North America and change the lives of the Indians in a dramatic way. With this new mobilization, the Indians no longer needed to rely on convenient hunting grounds. Their hunts led them far and wide across the west and by the time the first white explorers arrived in Jackson Hole, they undoubtedly encountered many trails criss-crossing this region, left by the Crows, Blackfeet, Nez Perce, Gros Ventre, Shoshone and Bannock Indians. The most profound changes were still yet to come.

In 1806, the Lewis and Clark Expedition was on their return journey from the Pacific back to St. Louis and civilization. Traveling with this group was a respected private and skilled hunter named John Colter. Colter desired to stay and explore this region for beaver (their pelts were valuable for the making of hats) and was granted a discharge from the expedition. He would surface in a myriad of factual and mythical accounts for several years to come.

Colter never kept a diary of his travels, but guessing from maps kept by Captain Clark - and later, Colter's own recollection - his journey, was indeed fantastic.

After spending one dismal year (as far as pelts were concerned,) trapping beaver, Colter began, under the direction of his newly found partner and friend, Manuel Lisa, an expedition to establish trade relations with the Indians. Equipped with meager provisions, (his intent was to live off the land) his gear consisted of one 30 pound pack, snowshoes, blankets and a shotgun with ammunition. Colter set out in late November for what was to be a 500 mile journey in the dead of winter. He was guessed to have entered Jackson Hole from the Gros Ventre Mountains to the east and it was there that Colter first beheld the full grandeur of the Tetons. Crossing the

EQUALITY ON THE NEW FRONTIER

As the citizenry of Jackson Hole achieved a more modern understanding of law and order, they began to realize the need for a more formalized government. In 1920 the citizens demonstrated their sense of equality by electing an all female slate-the first in U.S. history. Known as "the petticoat rulers" the women performed well-they were elected to a second term. One newspaper printed a poem entitled "New Rule of Queens".

Where once the powder
Smoke from "forty-fives"
Rose in the air to
Check our reckless lives;
Now powder puffs flash
Forth in dainty hand;
To rule the bad
Men of our land
And cowboy brave
And fighting men
All wilt before
The perfumed hand.

94

Teton Range by way of Teton Pass, he then traveled north through Pierre's Hole on the west side of the Tetons, stopping to carve his name and the date, 1808, on a stone referred to rather dubiously by some, as Colter's Stone. Colter's Stone is now on display at the park service museum in Moose. Recrossing the Tetons, he came upon the western shore of Yellowstone Lake and the many wonders of Yellowstone. He then followed the Yellowstone River up the Lamar Valley, back across the Absaroka Mountain Range, ending his remarkable journey. Upon his return the following spring, Colter's fantastic tales of towering pinnacled mountains, exploding geysers and boiling mud pots were met with disbelief and were quickly ridiculed as "Colter's Hell."

John Colter, the first white man to explore the picturesque valley of Jackson Hole and behold the treasures of Yellowstone, is truly one of the wests greatest frontiersman.

After Colter, many great explorers and trappers would come to Jackson Hole to claim their share of the abundance of beaver along the tributaries of the Snake River. Jim Bridger, Jedediah Smith, Bill Sublette and David E. Jackson are all synonymous with the term "mountain men." Davey Jackson, a trapper and founder of the Rocky Mountain Fur Company, loved this valley so much that his partner, Bill Sublette, named it after him; a hole being, at the time, any deep valley as seen from the rugged mountain passes. The "s" was later dropped, becoming simply Jackson Hole.

In 1832, silk hats became all the rage in Europe and fur trapping became a dying business in these parts. By the 1840's this valley became, once again, a place of peaceful solitude.

Coming over Teton Pass in the late 1800's, Jackson would not have been an impressive sight. You would have seen a untamed and remote valley dotted with homesteads, ranches and few downtown buildings. It was not an ideal place to raise a family. The Hole had become a hideout for outlaws, remittance men, trappers and lone cowboys and early pictures showed men outnumbered women two to one.

In 1889, the first Mormons arrived from Utah to settle in Jackson Hole and things began to change. The women were strong and tenacious and helped to tame and civilize this wild country. It was these Mormon emigrants that built the first schools in the valley, instituted the first post offices and founded Jackson Hole's first newspaper, the *Jackson's Hole Courier*. In 1920-1923, Jackson distinguished itself by electing the first all-woman town government in the United States.

With Yellowstone only 50 miles north as its neighbor, the valley of Jackson Hole soon became a romping grounds for tourists and a hunting mecca for wealthy sportsmen. Many visitors to the area felt that this

COLTER'S RUN

In the spring of 1808, John Colter, a former member of the Lewis and Clark Expedition, was trapping fur in the early morning hours with his fellow trapper John Potts. Suddenly, from the cliffs above, hundreds of Blackfeet Indian appeared, looking none too friendly. Not one to be called a coward, Potts took aim and killed one of the Indians in an act of resistance. He was promptly riddled with arrows and bullets. The blackfeet had not forgotten Colter from a previous battle with their enemy, the Crows. Colter had been traveling with the Crow Indians when a battle ensued between them and the Blackfeet. The Crows won, as they usually did, but Colter became a marked man by this act of treason. Back at the river the Blackfeet descended upon Colter, seized him and pulled him ashore where they disarmed and stripped him naked. It seems the Blackfeet were looking for an amusing way to kill their white enemy and Colter knew just enough of the Blackfeet language to know he was in serious trouble! He was told to run for his life and run he did. With the Blackfeet in pursuit, it's unlikely any man could have run faster than Colter did that day. With stones striking his body, he ran for the Jefferson River, some six miles away. Reaching a grove of cottonwoods about a mile from the river, he dared to look behind him and found one lone indian in hot pursuit. Colter whirled about to face him and the surprised indian stumbled and broke his spear. Seizing the moment, Colter instantly impaled the Blackfoot with his own spear and ran for the river. Plunging into the cold stream, Colter hid himself under brush and driftwood, watching as the Blackfeet search in vain for him the remainder of the day. After nightfall he escaped the icy stream and began his trek back to his post some 300 miles away. Without clothing for protection from the cold mountain nights or the blistering sun by day, Colter traveled in this manner for seven days. Without weapons to hunt, he arrived at his fort half starved, feet and body torn by cactus and barely alive.

Twice more colter would narrowly escape death at the hands of the Blackfeet. In 1810, discouraged from repeated losses of furs and supplies and close brushes with the Blackfeet, Colter left this area. He moved to Missouri where he married and purchased a small farm to live the remainder of his years. He died three years later from jaundice. The value of his estate at the time of his death was $229.41.

land should be permanently preserved and suggested that it become an extension to Yellowstone National Park. Yellowstone superintendent Horace Albright had also gazed south again and again at the awesome Tetons, dreaming of the day when Yellowstone would be expanded to include their beauty. "The best part of Yellowstone...yet not in the park," he was known to say. However, attempts to attach the Teton Mountains to Yellowstone were unsuccessful. In the meantime, farming flourished and ranches began sprouting up (some dude, some cattle) all over the valley. The beauty of the area was becoming seriously threatened by irrigation ditches, dams and unsightly tourist facilities. Despite opposition to this type of use, the government would not set aside this land for recreational use.

ESTABLISHING THE PARK

By 1926, the effects of development and exploitation of the region had grown considerably worse. The Forest Service permitted a telephone line to be stretched from the west side of Jenny Lake-Moran Road, thereby spoiling the view of the Tetons. The Forest Service was also considering offering part of the valley for sale to wealthy visitors and was planning to license commercial lumbering operations on Jackson Lake. A dance hall with a long row of cabins was built near the shore of Jenny Lake and a billboard was erected at the base of the Tetons proclaiming it to be the place of "The Hollywood Cowboy's Home." Jackson Hole seemed doomed to a land of unrestrained commercialism.

Dude ranching was a thriving industry in the 1920's and its sole survival depended on the preservation of the wild beauty of the valley. Afraid that a Park Service would bring unlimited paved roads, tourist facilities and crowds to the region, wranglers were opposed to annexing this region as part of the Park Service. It was Horace Albright who managed to convince prominent dude wrangler Struthers Burt that an extension of the Park Service, unlike the Forest Service, was the only way to protect the valley from commercial intrusion. Considerably discouraged already by the garish intrusions on the valley's wilderness areas, the dude industry decided to take a chance with Albright. A meeting between Albright and conservation proponents was held on July 26, 1923 at Maud Noble's cabin in Moose in order to draw up plans to protect the future of Jackson Hole. Their major obstacle to overcome was how to acquire the land they wanted to protect. Congress would not appropriate funds for the park annexation and business and land owners could not be expected to donate their land for the sake of preservation. What they needed were wealthy philanthropists willing to donate thousands of dollars for this recreational playground. For the next three years, Horace Albright promoted his plan for preservation to every wealthy tourist, journalist, editor, state official or congressman that would listen. It wasn't until 1926 that a wealthy philanthropist by the name of John D. Rockefeller would provide the generosity needed to realize a dream of a preserved paradise for the benefit of all.

HORACE ALBRIGHT (L) WITH HERBERT HOOVER (R), 1930

In 1926 Rockefeller was spending a 12-day vacation with his family in Yellowstone National Park, and accepted Albright's invitation for a drive south to view the valley of Jackson Hole. Albright revealed his dream to preserve the valley to Rockefeller. Disgusted with the sight of uncontrolled commercialism before him, Rockefeller asked Albright to come up with a cost for purchasing all the offensive properties in the valley. By the time Albright had accomplished this, Rockefeller informed him that his dream for Jackson Hole had grown even larger. To Albright's surprise, Rockefeller told him of his plan to purchase as much property as possible, which he would transfer ownership of to the Park Service. In order to buy the land at the most reasonable prices, Rockefeller formed the Snake River Land Company and land owners were not aware it was such a wealthy individual making offers on their land. A local banker by the name of Robert Miller was assigned as purchasing agent for the company and the whole process began.

It wasn't until 1930 that Albright and Rockefeller disclosed their plan to Congress and the residents of Jackson Hole. They were met with outrage. Anti-park groups, spear-headed by Senator Milward Simpson, (father of Senator Alan Simpson) charged a park service would be a major threat to the economy of the valley and ranchers would lose their grazing land. Under pressure from local opposition, Congress refused to accept Rockefeller's gift for more than a decade.

In 1943, President Roosevelt accepted the 32,000 acres offered by Rockefeller and added another 130,000 acres of Forest Service Land and dedicated it as the Jackson Hole National Monument. Park opponents fought to abolish this bill for several more years. It was not until 1947, when tourism began to flourish and revitalize the valley of Jackson Hole, that park opponents began to see the economic benefits of a recreational playground for its visitors. Finally, in 1950, a compromise was reached allowing ranchers life-long grazing rights on the land. After years of bitter controversy a dream was realized. It is now called Grand Teton National Park.

As it so often happens, the parks biggest opponents were reaping the rewards of Grand Teton National Park within only a few years.

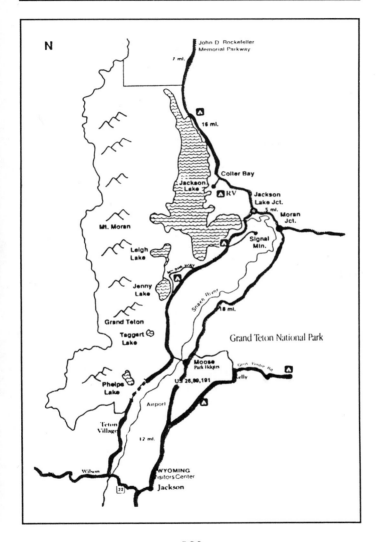

GRAND TETON
NATIONAL PARK
Visitor Information
P.O. Drawer 170
Moose, WY 83012
Telephone: (307) 733-2880

Highlight Attractions ☐ Teton National Park
☐ Menor's Ferry ☐ Around Jenny Lake ☐ Chapel of the
Transfiguration ☐ Around Jackson Lake ☐ Teton Science
School ☐ Gros Ventre Slide ☐ Cunningham Cabin
Fees: Entrance, $10.00 per vehicle or $4.00 for those entering
by bicycle or on foot.
Parking: Throughout the park.
Lodging: Colter Bay, Flagg Ranch Village, Jackson Lake
Lodge, Moose and Signal Mountain.
Restaurants and Cafeterias: Jackson Lake Lodge, Jenny Lake
Lodge and Signal Mountain.
Visitor Centers: Moose Visitor center and Colter Bay Visitor
Center.
Medical Services: Grand Teton Medical Clinic at Jackson Lake
Lodge.
Gift Shops: Colter Bay, Flagg Ranch Village, Jackson Lake
Lodge, Moose and Signal Mountain.

Service Stations: Colter Bay, Flagg Ranch, Jackson Lake Lodge, Jenny Lake Lodge, Moose and Signal Mountain.

Hiking: More than 200 miles of designated trails. Registration required for off-trail hiking.

Backpacking: Overnight trips require a non-fee permit.

Climbing: Must register at the Jenny Lake Ranger Station.

Bicycling: Only where cars can legally travel.

Horseback Riding: Jenny Lake, Jackson Lake Lodge, Colter Bay.

Campgrounds: Five park campgrounds. Advance reservations not accepted. Jenny Lake campground is for tents only.

Pets: Allowed on leashes, except in backcountry, on trails or in public buildings.

Activities in Grand Teton National Park: Hiking, fishing. camping, bicycling, boating, horseback riding, mountain climbing, snowmobiling and cross-country skiing.

TOURING GRAND TETON NATIONAL PARK

G rand Teton National Park is largely accessible by automobile, making it easy to drive the park within a day. All the drives you take in the park are scenic; wherever you go, the tantalizing views of the Teton Range are nearly inescapable.

The road system throughout Teton National Park consists of nearly 245 miles of dirt or paved roads. The main highway through Grand Teton National Park is U.S. 26-89-191. This road runs north and south and is open year round, although plowing ends near the south entrance to Yellowstone. For a more scenic drive, look for the Teton Park Road which begins at Moose junction near the south entrance of the park and ends at Jackson Lake junction. This paved road cuts toward the mountains and offers awe inspiring views. This road is not plowed in the winter, except for the southern end near Moose. The unplowed section of this road becomes a snowmobile cross-country ski route. Immediately south of Moose, a scenic winding nine mile road takes you to Teton Village. This road is narrow and rough in areas and RV's are not permitted. There are several scenic hiking trails that originate off this drive.

The highlights of the park that will be described here will begin as you enter the park at the visitor center at Moose, and will continue in a clock-wise direction around the park. Before starting out, I suggest you visit the visitor center for a brief orientation to the park's attractions.

Moose

☐ Moose Visitor Center

Stop here for a brief introduction to the parks many features. You will find a large selection of books, maps, photographs and slides to browse through. Don't forget to take a look at the controversial "Colter's Stone."

☐ Chapel of the Transfiguration

A dramatic and unique setting make this rustic chapel especially interesting. The tiny log structure was built during the summer of 1925 with funds and land donated by Miss Maud Noble. Above the alter is a large paned glass window, framing the awesome beauty of the Tetons. Services are held in the chapel every Sunday.

☐ Menor's Ferry

The ferry was constructed in 1872 by William Menor. Built to make crossing the river less hazardous, it served for many years as the primary way for early settlers to cross the Snake River.

☐ Taggart Lake

After leaving the Menor's Ferry area, continue northwest along the park road approximately 2 miles until you arrive at the Taggart Lake Trailhead. Visitor parking is on the left.

The lake was named after W.R. Taggart, a member of the Hayden Expedition. Like Jenny Lake and other lakes along foot of the Tetons, it was created when glacier moraines created dams that formed the lakes. This very popular hike has a distance of four miles round-trip. **Bradley Lake** can be seen by taking a 2 mile side-loop trail that bears off to the northwest from the Taggart Lake Trailhead.

☐ Jenny Lake Area

Approximately 8 miles from Taggart Lake, a scenic one way loop road will take you south to String Lake. This narrow pretty lake connects Jenny Lake with Leigh Lake. There is a scenic path around its shoreline. Across the lake are some of the most exceptional views of the **Cathedral Group**: Teewinot, Grand Teton and Mt. Owen. A short, level hike will lead you to **Leigh Lake**, a scenic glacial lake with a nice sandy beach.

The second largest and most popular lake in the park is Jenny Lake. It is named after the Shoshone wife of Dick Leigh, for whom Leigh Lake is named. The lake is ringed with an emerald green necklace of lodgepole

THE CATHEDRAL GROUP

109

pine, spruce and fir. It is in the interior of this lush forest that you will savor your most memorable images. There are a cornucopia of nature trails criss-crossing this favorite section of the park; **Inspiration Point** being the most popular. It is located on the far side (west) of Jenny Lake and can be reached by a 2 mile hike from the Jenny Lake Ranger Station or you can ride one of the shuttle boats that carry visitors across the lake every 20 minutes. The cost is $3.00 RT for adults and $1.75 for children. Once you arrive at the dock, climb the trail ½ mile to **Hidden Falls**. This is actually a cascade that plunges some 250 feet from a bench along Cascade Creek. Continue the trail another ¼ mile as it climbs to Inspiration Point, some 400 feet above Jenny Lake. This will provide you with an excellent view of Jackson Hole to the east. Most hikers stop at this point, worn out from the steep climb, not realizing that the next few miles into **Cascade Canyon** are a breeze. Here you will find incredible views of the Grand Teton, thick forests and lush green meadows.

For a longer trek around Jenny Lake's shoreline, pick up the 6½ mile trail anywhere along the eastern shore of the lake. A good starting point would be across from the Jenny Lake Lodge.

HIDDEN FALLS

111

☐ Jenny Lake Lodge

Located on the one-way loop road, this picturesque little lodge is nestled in a large alpine meadow. It offers nicely decorated cabins and good dining. The Sunday breakfast buffet is a special treat not to be missed.

☐ Signal Mountain

North from Jenny Lake Junction, take the Teton Park Road northeast about 4 miles to Signal Mountain Road. (No RV's or trailers permitted.) This five mile road climbs nearly 1,000 feet to the summit of Signal Mountain, providing one of the most awe-inspiring vistas anywhere. This is an excellent area to view **The Potholes**, a deeply pitted area created when huge chunks of ice were left behind by retreating glaciers. As the ice melted, large depressions, or pothole, were left on the valley floor.

☐ Signal Mountain Lodge

Sitting on the banks of Jackson Lake is Signal Mountain Lodge. The lodge offers accommodations, dining, gift shop and bar in a spectacular setting.

☐ Chapel of the Sacred Heart

Back on Teton Park Road, the road continues a short distance before you see the Chapel of the Sacred Heart. This Roman Catholic Church is used for weekly mass. Adjacent to the church is a nice picnic area overlooking Jackson Lake.

Jackson Lake Area

☐ Jackson Lake Dam

The Teton Park Road ends at Jackson Lake Junction. Just before the junction the road passes the dam. The controversial dam was completed in 1916 to impound water for Idaho potato farmers. The 70 foot dam raised the natural water level of Jackson Lake 39 feet, flooding over 7,000 acres and leaving behind a mess of floating trees and debris. With the first dam in place, farmers in neighboring states were now optimistic that future dams could be built on Jenny and Leigh Lakes as well. Fortunately, this never came into fruition. It was already bad enough that something so unnatural was built on the shores of one of the most beautiful lakes in the world. The Jackson Lake Dam underwent a 82-million-dollar renovation project in 1988, greatly improving its look.

☐ Willow Flats

After turning north on U.S. Route 89, the Willow Flats Turnout will provide you with splendid views over the flats. This is a good area for sighting moose, especially in the early morning hours.

☐ Jackson Lake

You could put all the six major lakes ringing the base of the Teton Range into the seventh, Jackson Lake. The largest in the park, the lake is 17 miles long and is 25,730 acres in size. With the Tetons as a backdrop, this

JACKSON LAKE

is a particularly beautiful area to stretch your legs beside the lake's rocky shoreline.

☐ Jackson Lake Lodge

As you continue north along Route 89, you will come to a side road that leads to the Jackson Lake Lodge. Built by the Rockefellers' in 1950, it sits on a small bluff overlooking the beauty of Jackson Lake. The lodge is worth a visit if only for a look at the views from the main lounge. A huge 60-foot high window frames an incredible view of **Mt. Moran**'s massive flat summit, resting behind the blue waters of Jackson Lake.

The lodge offers accommodations, good dining and shopping.

North to Yellowstone

☐ Emma Matilda Lake and Two Ocean Lake

Directly across from the Jackson Lake Lodge side road, is the turn off to Emma Matilda Lake and Two Ocean Lake. The trip to both lakes is 14 miles round-trip and takes you through splendid wooded wildlife areas. There are a variety of good hikes in this area.

☐ Colter Bay Village

Further north up the main road, you'll arrive at Colter Bay Village, a highly developed section of the park containing cabins, a marina with boat rentals, general store, service station and the main attraction; the **Colter Bay Indian**

Arts Museum. Named after hunter and trapper John Colter, the museum houses the David T. Vernon collection of Indian pieces. The collection includes ceremonial masks, pipes, beaded textiles, shields and kachina dolls, all thought to be some of the finest pieces in any national park. The museum is open daily from 8-5:00 p.m. from May through September and 8-7:00 p.m. in mid-summer.

Jackson Lake to Moran Junction
☐ Oxbow Bend
Heading southeast from the Jackson Lake Junction the road passes over Oxbow Bend. This section of the river has formed an arc-shaped lake, caused by the meandering of the Snake River. This is a favorite spot for artists, photographers and naturalists because of its beauty and abundance of wildlife. It is a ideal spot to see moose, pelicans, sandhill cranes, blue heron geese, ducks and an occasional trumpeter swan.

South to Jackson
☐ Cunningham Cabin
About 5 miles south of Moran Junction on U.S.26-89-191, is Cunningham Cabin. The cabin was once the home of J. Pierce Cunningham, who homesteaded the property in 1885. The site gained its notoriety when an example of

"frontier justice" was acted out here in 1893. According to historians, two men who had been permitted to winter there were suspected of being horse thieves because of the strange brandings on their horses. A posse of vigilantes surrounded the cabin and the two men were shot. It was later believed that the two men were innocent of any wrong-doing.

☐ Triangle X Ranch

Approximately 1 mile south of Cunningham Cabin is the turn-off to Triangle X Ranch. The ranch is the most famous of any dude ranch in Jackson Hole, having been managed by the Turner family for the past 60 years.

☐ Blacktail Butte

The butte is another example of the effects of debris left behind by retreating glaciers. It is a former habitat area for blacktail or mule deer. Rock climbers can often be seen climbing the butte's limestone ledges.

☐ Teton Science School

Nestled in a small valley along Ditch Creek, is the Teton Science School. The school was founded in 1967 and offers a year-round spectrum of courses relating to the Teton Range and wilderness topics. There are classes available for all ages, from children's elementary school level courses to adult college level courses. Subjects include botany, geology, identifying animal tracks, wildlife photography, wolf recovery and an excellent 30-day

Emergency Medical Trainee wilderness course. Consider a 3-5 day educational seminar during your stay in the valley. You can obtain a free copy of the course catalog by calling (307) 733-4765.

The Gros Ventre Slide (pronounced grow-vahnt)
This astounding portrayal of nature's tremendous force is considered to be one of largest earth movements in the world. On June 23, 1925, 50 million cubic yards of earth, rock and debris began a slide from an altitude of 9,000 feet. This movement lasted only a few moments, but when it was finished a river below would become instantly dammed and the landscape changed forever. Believed to be caused by heavy rains, the slide plunged down and across the Gros Ventre River, forming a dam 225 feet high and nearly ½ mile wide, creating what is now appropriately called, Slide Lake. Part of this dam gave way two years later, sending a wall of water, mud and rock flowing down the canyon, destroying everything in its path. The town of Kelly was nearly wiped out by the flood and six people lost their lives.

Follow the walking trail out to the middle of the dam and see for yourself the magnitude of this occurrence. **Directions from Jackson:** Take Highway 89 North to Gros Ventre Junction, then go right (east) through the town of Kelly. Turn right again on Gros Ventre Road. This will take you to the slide.

Where to Find the Wildlife

O n any given day in Grand Teton National Park, it is possible to see deer, moose, elk, bison, bear, Bighorn sheep and a variety of waterfowl.

Some of these animals are more difficult to find than others. The most common mammal to spot in the park is the **elk**. It is most often at midlevel elevations in the summer and on the National Elk refuge in the winter. Though scarce, the **bison** can be found in the northern areas such as Moran and Buffalo Valley. Look for **moose** in the mountains, in willow patches and near ponds, especially in the Oxbow Bend area and at Sawmill Ponds. **Pronghorn sheep** can be spotted in Antelope Flats and mule deer will be found throughout the park. **Bighorn sheep** frequent the higher elevations of the park such as the upper slopes of the Tetons. The **grizzly** and **black bear** are not common in Teton National Park, but could be encountered just about

119

anywhere. It is important to remember that you should **stay at least 300 feet from large animals**, especially bears. Never come between an adult and her offspring.

The Oxbow Bend area is an excellent area to look for waterfowl. Most common are **pelicans, ospreys, bald eagles** and a variety of ducks. The slow-moving water of the Oxbow is also a prime habitat area for **beavers, river otters and muskrats.** The Snake River is noted for the celebrated **cutthroat trout** and its other fishes are natural prey for **Canadian Geese, trumpeter swans and great blue herons**.

LODGING IN TETON NATIONAL PARK
Hotels, Lodges and Cabins

Lodge	Rate	Facilities
Colter Bay Jackson Lake (307) 543-2855	$17-$48	AAA approved. Cabins and tents
Jackson Lake Lodge Jackson Lake (307) 543-2855	$65+	AAA approved. Pool.
Jenny Lake Lodge Jenny Lake (307) 733-4647	$205	AAA approved. Rate includes breakfast and dinner. Very nice.
Signal Mountain Lodge Jackson Lake (307) 543-2831	$60+	AAA approved. Cottages with kitchenettes.
Hatchett Motel	$50	AAA approved. Clean, rustic motel.

CAMPGROUNDS

The following campgrounds are available for a fee of $8.00 per night. With the exception of Jenny Lake, all campgrounds will allow tents, trailers and RVs. The Jenny Lake Campground is open to tents and small trailers only. There are no utility hookups available at any of the campgrounds.

Colter Bay and Flagg Ranch Trailer Villages offer facilities with full hook-ups, showers and laundry. Reserve in advance.

Campground	Dates ('93)	Sites	Features
Jenny Lake	5/23-10/19	49	Tents or small camping vehicles only. No trailers.
Gros Ventre	5/23-9/28	360	Dumping station.
Signal Mountain	5/9-10/13	86	Dumping station.
Colter Bay	5/23-10-28	310	Dumping station. Showers, laundry, propane.
Lizard Creek	6/13-9/8	60	

ACTIVITIES
IN THE PARKS
& JACKSON HOLE

HIKING

W hether you are strolling a little stretch of the winding Snake River, climbing steep, rocky moraines to find a hidden lake shimmering emerald green against the backdrop of the majestic Tetons or ambling through a thick, mossy forest, you'll discover the most intimate and rewarding details of this wondrous area on foot. Some hiking enthusiast spend their entire vacations on these trails and fortunately, the area is rich with trails for every inclination: mountaintop trails, river trails, forested trails, lake trails, wildlife trails and canyon trails.

There are more than 1,000 miles of marked trails in Yellowstone National Park and 200 miles of trails in Grand Teton National Park. These nature walks offer vistas of lush alpine meadows, tumbling prismatic waterfalls, magnificent geysers and thermal areas, abundant wildlife and unbelievable forest fire areas.

Not only is this the ultimate way to enjoy a communion with nature, it also provides you with a sense of freedom experienced from the absence of civilization. Nature is the ruler here. While you enjoy the beauty of a tumbling waterfall one instant, the next may find you contemplating the perils of fording a mountain stream tumbling over slippery river rocks. There is a certain feeling of satisfaction that is achieved when one feels the impact of not being in control of his or her environment. Without this struggle to manipulate and control your surroundings comes a feeling of perspective about yourself and a sense of peaceful acceptance. I'm convinced that if more people took up hiking as a hobby, the ever-popular self-help book would become a thing of the past.

So go ahead and stretch you legs on one of the many hiking trails in the valley: it may become the highlight of your trip. For an added experience, pack a lunch and wile away the whole afternoon. You'll come away re-awakened to what clean mountain air and beautiful surroundings really feel like!

The vast wilderness of Teton and Yellowstone National Parks contain some hazards not commonly encountered anywhere else. While you need not fear backcountry hiking, a little common sense goes a long way. Yellowstone backcountry is also grizzly country and because a startled bear is a dangerous bear, you should always make noise when hiking. Whistling or carrying bear bells and hiking during the daylight hours will reduce your chances of surprising a bear on your path. If you are caught in a situation where you are face to face with a grizzly, the following methods will help to minimize your risk of injury.

BEAR FACTS

- Make noise when hiking by carrying bear bells, whistling or talking loudly.
- Avoid carrying odorous foods.
- Do not approach any dead carcass. It may be a recent kill and the bear may still be in the area defending his property.

Though you chances of encountering a grizzly are very rare, (there are no more than 250 in Yellowstone) here are methods to reduce your risk of injury.

- Don't run. This will only incite the bear to pursue you and bears can run at speeds up to 30 mile per hour.
- Remain calm and slowly move to the nearest tree and begin to climb it. Grizzlies have difficulty climbing trees (though black bears are expert climbers). To distract the bear while you do this, throw down any things you may be carrying such as a backpack or clothing. Hopefully, the bear may choose to inspect these items instead of pursuing you.
- If there are no trees in the area, it is best to "play dead." Assume a "cannonball" position; curling up to protect your face and stomach while playing dead.

The most dangerous animal that you are more likely to encounter is a moose. They are known to have nasty dispositions and, depending the season, can be quite aggressive. Allow a wide berth for any moose that is approaching or lying nearby. Should a moose begin to charge you, you should run to the nearest protective cover such as behind a large boulder or tree, since a moose can easily outrun you over open ground.

Yellowstone's thermal areas should be treated with caution and respect. Don't hike in thermal areas after dark and never hike over an area that is completely void of plant life.

There are a few "do's" and even fewer "don'ts" involved with hiking in wilderness and mountainous areas. The following list should help make your hiking experience a more enjoyable one:

DO

1.) DO bring along a water bottle. At higher elevations, it is easy to experience the effects of dehydration.

2.) DO bring along a warm sweater or protective rain gear. Sudden storms could arise and at high elevations, could lead to hyperthermia.

3.) DO wear comfortable walking shoes.

4.) DO be aware of weather conditions the day of your hike.

5.) DO stay on the trails. Not only does this prevent erosion, it may also prevent you from getting lost. Always observe the warnings of cautionary signs when hiking in thermal areas.

6.) DO let someone know your itinerary and when to expect you back.
7.) If you are an avid bird watcher, animal watcher or whatever, DO bring along a set of binoculars.

DON'T

1.) DON'T approach the wildlife. They may seem tame, but if you lean towards the overly curious or naive you may end up being the subject of one of those amusing (or not so amusing) tourist stories on the cover of the Jackson Hole Guide.
2.) DON'T drink water from streams or lakes. Even though the water appears to be clean, many lakes and streams contain bacteria, viruses and microscopic organisms called giardiasis.
3.) Don't leave marked trails unless you are a very experienced hiker. Special permission must be received from park rangers before undertaking such a trip.

YELLOWSTONE HIKES

The following trails were chosen because they are relatively short day-hikes, because of their low level of difficulty and for their scenic value. With over 1,000 miles of trails in the park, this is obviously just a tiny sampling. There are several very good topographical maps and hiking books available at the Yellowstone's visitor centers including *"Hiking the Yellowstone Backcountry,"* by Orville E. Bach and *"Day Hiking Yellowstone,"* by Tom Carter.

HIKES IN THE LOWER LOOP

BISCUIT BASIN/MYSTIC FALLS

Start: 2 miles North of the Old Faithful interchange. Park in the Biscuit Basin parking area.
End: Same as start
Distance: 3.5 miles
Hiking time: 2 hours
Level of difficulty: Easy
Description: From the parking area, take the wooden walkway across the Firehole River to the far side of Biscuit Basin. Continue until the trail leaves the boardwalk and enters the forest. This trail will gradually climb for the next mile to the base of Mystic Falls. As you walk along the Firehole River, notice the effects of the 1988 fires that ripped through this area. The wildflowers are superb along the way; especially noticeable are the Indian Paintbrush. After the falls, the trail continues to the right along a series of switchbacks to the Madison Plateau. From this vantage point you'll be able to view the entire Geyser Basin. If you're lucky, or simply patient enough, you'll witness one of these magnificent eruptions. See if you can spot Old Faithful. Hint: The Old Faithful Inn is located to the right of the geyser! Continue along the trail. It will drop back down to the valley floor and merge back with the Mystic Falls Trail, which will lead you back to the Biscuit Basin parking area.

STORM POINT

Start: 3 miles east of Lake Junction, toward the East Entrance Gate. The trailhead is located on the south side of the road.

End: Same as beginning

Distance: 2 miles

Hiking time: 1-2 hours

Level of difficulty: Easy

Description: This hike will provide you with a spectacular view of Yellowstone Lake and an opportunity to spot some of the wildlife of the lake region: moose, waterfowl and marmots. Follow the trail south from the highway around the western edge of Indian Pond; an ancient crater cased by a sudden, violent explosion of steam. After the trail reaches Yellowstone Lake, it then begins to parallel the shore to the right as it continues to Storm Point. Storm Point was aptly named. The fierce winds here come from the southwest, creating huge waves that crash against the rocky shore. Notice the extensive erosion that has occurred along the lake's shore, a testament to the relentless winds and powerful waves of Lake Yellowstone. You will follow the same trail back to your car.

FAIRY FALLS

Start: Firehole River Bridge, located off the Grand Loop Road via a short spur road 4½ miles north of the Old Faithful overpass.

End: Same as beginning

Distance: 6.4 miles, roundtrip

Hiking time: 4-5 hours roundtrip

Level of difficulty: Easy to moderate

Description: After you cross the steel bridge across the Firehole river, look for a small road on the west side of the highway. Take this short road about 0.2 miles to the beginning of the trailhead. The trail passes through the Madison Plateau and leads you along a series of colorful springs and geysers. One of the most impressive is Grand Prismatic, located on the right of the trail. The yellow, green and red colors are due to the heavy concentration of algae that thrives in the warm temperature of the spring. At the one-mile marker, the trail veers left and enters the forest. This area was severely burned by the 1988 fires, but close inspection will reveal lodgepole pine seedlings and a variety of grasses. At the 2.5 mile marker you reach Fairy Falls. The graceful fall plunges 197 feet to a small pool below. If you would like to continue another ½ mile down the same trail, you will reach the Imperial Geyser. It rises out of a large crater that measures about 150 feet across. Eruptions, although infrequent, reach a height of 40 feet.

SHOSHONE LAKE TRAIL

Start: Just east of DeLacy Creek off the Grand Loop Road, approximately 9½ miles east of Old Faithful.

End: Lone Star Geyser

Distance: 14 miles roundtrip

Hiking time: 8-10 hours

Level of difficulty: Moderate

Description: The trail, named DeLacey Creek Trail, runs south from the road and follows DeLacy Creek to the shore of Shoshone Lake. This is a perfect area for spotting moose, elk and Sandhill Cranes. If you've not seen a Sandhill Crane, you are in for a surprise. These birds stand as tall as mule deer and have a wingspan of over 6 feet. Listen for their shrill cries as you hike along. Most of the trail passes through dense forest until you reach the lake at the 3 mile marker. Here, the trail divides. Turn right and follow the trail along the lakes shoreline. The next two miles will afford many spectacular views of Shoshone Lake. You will pass several excellent campsites along this route. When you reach the 5 mile marker, the trail veers back into the forest until you reach the 7 mile marker. A ranger station is located here, but seldom is anyone on duty. Return via the same trail.

RIDDLE LAKE TRAIL

Start: At the South Entrance Road, approximately 4.2 miles south of Grant Village.

End: Same as beginning.

Distance: 4 miles roundtrip

Hiking time: 3-4 hours

Level of difficulty: Easy

Description: This short, easy hike reaches the lake in just 2 miles. It is a popular spot for fisherman because of its large population of cutthroat trout.

Before this region was explored, it was believed that a lake existed in Yellowstone that provided major drainage to both oceans. In the 1870's, it was learned that a stream draining from the lake crosses the Continental Divide and the "riddle" was solved. The trail will cross the Continental Divide 0.2 miles into the hike.

133

HIKES IN THE UPPER LOOP
MOUNT WASHBURN
Start: 5 miles north of Canyon Village at Dunraven Pass. Look for a parking area on the east side of the road.

End: Same as beginning

Distance: 5.5 miles roundtrip

Hiking time: 4-5 hours

Level of difficulty: Moderate

Description: By far, one of the nicest and most popular day-hikes in Yellowstone. Because of its elevation (10,243) and central location in the park, the vista from the observation tower on the top of Mount Washburn is one of the most spectacular. In 1885, naturalist John Muir described Mount Washburn in this way:

> *'Climb the mountains and get their good tidings. Nature's peace will flow into you as sunshine flows into trees. The winds will blow their own freshness into you and the storms their energy, while cares will drop off like autumn leaves.'*
>
> *John Muir*

Park in the parking area and begin the ascent by following the old road bed. This road was originally constructed in the 1920's to allow stagecoaches and Model-T Fords to reach the summit. This is an excellent opportunity to view wildflowers such as the vibrant red tops of Indian Paintbrush (Wyoming's state flower) and the purple and blue pea-like flowers called lupine. Frequently spotted near the top are summering bands of bighorn sheep. Once on top, look for the impressive view of the Grand Canyon of the Yellowstone. You'll also be able to see Hayden Valley, Yellowstone Lake to the south and on a clear day, the Tetons may be visible. Be sure to spend some time studying the TOPO map displayed at the observation tower. It will help familiarize you with the various mountain ranges, lakes and valleys of the region. Return by using the same trail.

CANYON RIM

Start: At the Yellowstone canyon view area named "Grandview" located on the North Rim Road.
End: Artist point
Distance: 3.7 miles one way
Hiking time: 3 hours
Level of difficulty: Moderate
Description: This trail runs along the rim of the magnificent Grand Canyon of the Yellowstone, affording stunning views of the canyon's colorful 1,200 foot walls: flaming red, pastel pink, yellow and brilliant orange. From the Grandview parking area, follow the North Rim Trail upriver as it hugs the rim of the canyon. When you see the spray from the Upper Falls in the distance, you will notice a switchback trail that leads down to the Lower Falls. Start down this switchback and continue straight at

135

the first switchback. You will soon cross Cascade Creek above Crystal Falls. At the 1.25 mile marker, you will arrive at the Upper Falls parking area. Continue a short distance further upstream and use the highway bridge to cross the Yellowstone River. Immediately after crossing the bridge, turn left and take the South Rim Trail downstream as it continues along the river. At the 2.5 mile marker you will reach a directing sign for Uncle Tom's Trail, which will lead you down the most breathtaking trail in the canyon.

TOWER FALL
Start: 2.5 miles southeast of Tower Junction in the Tower Falls parking area.
End: Same as beginning
Distance: 2.5 miles
Hiking time: 1.5 hours
Level of difficulty: Easy
Description: Tower Fall is one of Yellowstone's most popular attractions. This trail will take you along a scenic portion of the Yellowstone River and on to the base of the 132 foot fall, providing you with a completely different and equally impressive view. To the right of the Tower Fall overlook, a well defined trail begins a switchback down to the base of the fall. Near the bottom, the trail will divide. Follow the trail left to the base of the fall. The trail to the

right will lead you to the bank of the Yellowstone River. Notice the steep slopes of **Specimen Ridge** just across the river.

TETON HIKES

The following trails represent a small sample of the more than 200 miles of diverse trails available in the park. For a more complete listing and to learn about any special weather advisories, visit the Jenny Lake Ranger Station or the visitor center in Moose.

The most popular hikes in the park are centered around the Teton's many canyons and lakes. These trails are usually in good condition, however unexpected floods, especially during the melting season which can last as late as July, will occasionally make for muddy conditions.

AMPHITHEATER LAKE TRAIL
Start: Lupine Meadows parking area
End: Same as beginning
Distance: 9.6 miles roundtrip
Level of difficulty: Strenuous
Description: This is a steep but manageable hike that climbs 3,000 feet to an elevation of 9,700 feet for wonderful views of Jackson Hole. Amphitheater Lake sits just below Disappointment Peak, a 11,618 foot peak named by mountain climbers who mistakenly thought they had scaled the face of the Grand Teton.

CASCADE CANYON TRAIL
Start: Jenny Lake boat dock
End: Lake Solitude
Distance: 8.5 miles one way
Level of difficulty: Moderate to strenuous
Description: This very popular trail offers something for everybody; sparkling waterfalls, canyons with towering peaks, dense forests and alpine lakes.

CUNNINGHAM CABIN TRAIL
Start: Begins near the cabin, 6 miles south of Moran
End: Same as beginning
Distance: .5 mile roundtrip
Level of difficulty: Easy
Description: This trail features early ranching history of Jackson Hole and a walk through a historical homesite.

COLTER BAY TRAIL
Start: .5 mile from Colter Bay Visitor Center
End: Same as beginning
Distance: .5 mile roundtrip
Level of difficulty: Easy
Description: This loop trail leads you through dense forests along Jackson Lake to a panoramic view of the Tetons.

LEIGH LAKE TRAIL
Start: String Lake picnic area
End: Bear Paw Lake
Distance: 7 miles roundtrip
Level of difficulty: Easy
Description: This trip closely parallels Leigh Lake with views of Indian Paintbrush Canyon.

LUNCH TREE HILL TRAIL
Start: Jackson Lake Lodge parking area
End: Same as beginning
Distance: 5 miles roundtrip
Level of difficulty: Easy to moderate
Description: A magnificent trail, used considerably by John D. Rockefeller and noted for being the inspiration behind his massive land purchase. Several wayside exhibits provide information along the way.

OXBOW BEND TRAIL
Start: At trailhead located down a short side road, 3 miles east of Jackson Lake Junction.
End: Same as beginning
Distance: 1 mile roundtrip
Level of difficulty: Easy
Description: Winds along the Snake River with plenty of opportunity to view moose and waterfowl.

CROSS-COUNTRY SKIING

Cross-country skiers will delight in the trails and the backcountry skiing opportunities available in the valley and national parks. In Yellowstone, marked trails are located throughout the Upper Geyser Basin, Tower Fall, Canyon area and Mammoth Hot Springs. There are a profusion of trails in Grand Teton National Park that can be enjoyed by those with little or no experience in cross-country skiing. Most trails are either level or gently sloping, although a few will provide challenge for the more experienced skier.

General recreation maps are available from the park's visitor centers. For an excellent topographical map, I highly recommend the free cross-country ski-guide available through Skinny Skis, located at 65 W. Deloney.

The most scenic and popular cross-country ski area near Jackson, is Grand Teton National Park. The region will afford you a spectacular setting with level terrain and easy gentle slopes. The most popular tours in the park are the **Jenny Lake** and **Taggart Lake** tours. They are located 12 miles north of Jackson via highway 89. Turn left at Moose and continue 3½ miles to the **Taggart Lake Trailhead**. The trail to Taggart Lake is an easy 3 miles roundtrip with the trail marked with orange flagging. To take the Jenny Lake tour, continue on the park road ¼ mile past the Taggart Lake parking area. The plowed section of the road ends at the Cottonwood Creek bridge. The route to Jenny Lake is 9 miles roundtrip and the terrain fairly flat. The views of the Tetons are superb.

From Teton Village, head north 1 mile on the **Moose-Wilson Road** until you reach the unplowed section of the road. Park here. The trail can be followed for several miles toward Moose as it passes through scenic aspen groves and lodgepole pine forests. For the more experienced skier, take the **Granite Canyon Trail** 1 mile up the road. Stay within the foothills of the canyon if you are unaware of the current avalanche conditions.

For cross-country skiing in the immediate vicinity of Jackson, check out the **Cache Creek Canyon** tour. Drive to the east end of Cache Creek Drive until it dead-ends at a parking lot. This is a gradual uphill, then downhill tour. Be careful when rounding corners, as snowmobilers use this route also.

Ski-rental companies throughout the valley offer guided back-country excursions with equipment rental or you can rent just the equipment and go off on your own. Rental fees range from $8.00 to $10.00 for adults for 1 full day and about $7.00 for children. Half day rates are also available. If you require a ski-instructor, plan on paying between $15 and $25 per hour.

141

For more information, you may contact the following companies:

►**Jack Dennis Sports:** (307) 733-3270
50 E. Broadway, south side of Town Square
►**Skinny Skis:** (307) 733-6094
65 W. Deloney
►**Teton Mountaineering:** (307) 733-3595
86 E. Broadway
►**Togwotee Mountain Lodge**: (800) 543-2847
or 543-2847,
►**Trails End Ranch:** (307) 733-1616

MOUNTAIN CLIMBING

While mountain climbing is *not* for the average visitor who comes to the park, it is easy to understand why veteran climbers travel from around the world to climb these peaks. In the world of climbing, the Teton Range is considered one of the premier areas in the nation. Several thousand people have scaled the Tetons to registered their names at the rocky summit. The most popular climb is The Grand. It has 27 different routes to the summit (13,766 feet) offering various degrees of difficulty, but all routes are steep and full of challenge even for the best of climbers.

Mountain climbing requires a special permit from the Jenny Lake Ranger station. If you would like to attend one of the intensive full day climbing schools to learn how to begin your own climb, there are two excellent climbing schools located in Jackson Hole. These companies offer climbing instruction for all degrees of difficulty, from basic climbing techniques to snow climbing in the high mountain passes. You can enroll in the **Exum School of American Guides**, tele: 733-2297, located at Jenny Lake or **Jackson Hole Mountain Guides**, tele: 733-4979, located at 165 N. Glenwood, in downtown Jackson. Both are park-approved. It is advisable to make your reservations for classes several months in advance if you want to scale the Grand. The cost for a two-day guided climb to the Grand's summit (including food, and gear) is around $400. "It's a favorite trip of people who may not want to be climbers for the rest of their life, but who do want to climb the Grand," said Dean Moore, of Exum Patrol.

TAKING A RIDE
Saddle-up!

While the Old West depended on horses for basic transportation, today horseback riding is for pure riding enjoyment; an opportunity to amble down a dusty trail and imagine a simpler era. Horseback is still the most classic, and sometimes the only practical, way to enjoy these remote wilderness areas. In Jackson Hole, there are plenty of places to rent your own four legged friend. Your options seem to be limitless in this activity; you can head out on a gentle buckskin or a perky Palomino for an hour or a week. Many ranches, lodges and resorts located throughout the valley and at the entrances to Teton and Yellowstone National Parks allow you to choose from a range of equestrian options: from brief hour-long excursions to day long mountain trips to guided, week-long wilderness pack trips into the remote wilderness areas. The experienced outfitters will pack you and your gear into the rugged beauty of the western "outback", prepare several hearty, if simple, meals and show off their knowledge of the valley's trees, flowers, mountain ranges, historical sites and abundant wildlife.

To determine what riding experience is best for you, your budget and your time allowance, talk to a few of the dozen or so local outfitters and equestrian centers listed here and....Happy Trails!

144

HORSEBACK RIDING IN YELLOWSTONE
►Mammoth Hot Springs
Provides 1-hour trail rides only at a rate of $11.85 per person. Open mid-May through mid-September. For reservations, call (307) 344-7311.
►Canyon Lodge
Provides 1-hour and 2-hour trail rides. Children must be 8 years or older and measure 4 feet tall. Open mid-June through mid-August. For reservations, call (307)344-7311.
►Roosevelt Lodge
Provides 1 and 2-hour trail rides, Stagecoach rides and Old West Dinner Cookouts. For reservation, call (307) 344-7311.

HORSEBACK RIDING IN TETON
►Jackson Lake Lodge Corral
Trail rides of all lengths. Prices start at $10 for 1 hour to $45 for the entire day. Weight limit is 250 lbs. Breakfast and evening rides available. Open mid-May through September. (307) 543-2811 or (800) 628-9988

►Teton Trail Rides, Inc.
Located at Jenny Lake. Rides of various lengths through the Tetons. Guide service, pack trips, meals available. Rates are from $10 for 1 hour to $45 for the entire day. Open June through September. (307) 733-2108

145

▶Colter Bay Village Corral
Trail rides of various lengths. Breakfast and evening rides, wagon seats available. Open Mid-May through September. (307) 543-2811

HORSEBACK RIDING IN JACKSON
▶Bar-T-5
Located at 850 Cache Creek Rd., Jackson. Covered wagon cook-out and wild-west show with singing cowboys, Indians and mountain men. Prices for adults, including food and entertainment, is $26.98, children 9-14 is $16.98 and children 4-8 is $13.98. Children under three are free. Reservations are required. 733-5386.
▶Snow King Stables
Options include breakfast rides, cookouts and more. Located at 400 East Snow King Ave., Jackson. 733-5781.
▶Spring Creek Equestrian Center
No rides, lessons only. Lessons are $35. 739-9062.
Stagecoach Rides
If no steed is tame enough for your liking - or you simply yearn for a more elegant form of horsing around, try the summer carriage tours through downtown Jackson. It's a charming way to experience a little taste of western culture. Stagecoach rides are available from Memorial Day weekend to Labor Day and can be found on the southwest corner of the Town Square.

◆ ◆ ◆ ◆ ◆ ◆ ◆ ◆ ◆ ◆ ◆ ◆ ◆ ◆ ◆ ◆ ◆ ◆

Snowmobile Regulations

•Operators must be 16 years or older

•Children under 12 may operate only if
accompanied by an adult.

•Possession of an open container or bota bags
is illegal.

•Wildlife has the right of way. Approaching
animals is prohibited.

◆ ◆ ◆ ◆ ◆ ◆ ◆ ◆ ◆ ◆ ◆ ◆ ◆ ◆ ◆ ◆ ◆ ◆

Snowmobiling

J ackson Hole and the national park systems have
long been known as prime snowmobile country
and it's fast becoming one of the areas favorite
winter recreational activities. With Yellowstone
and most of Teton limited in the winter months
to over-snow vehicles, it is one of the only ways
to travel so far and so fast over the snow blanketed
alpine wilderness. January and February, when the area
gets its greatest snowfall, are good months to sample the

147

wonders of this wide-open land with its frozen lakes, icy meadows and steaming geysers. Yellowstone offers tours along the rim of the Grand Canyon of the Yellowstone, the West Thumb thermal basin or the Old Faithful area, which also offers accommodations. There are literally hundreds of miles of groomed trails throughout Yellowstone, and all gateway towns offer snowmobile rentals. This is an excellent area for viewing wildlife that come to graze along the warm thermal basins. However, animals are especially sensitive in the winter months. Approaching too closely will force them to move away, expending much-needed energy that's needed to survive the harsh winter. Allow animals the right of way when you encounter them along the roadside. Environmental studies **do** indicate that the animals become stressed by the presence and noise of these machines.

Grand Teton National Park offers many accessible and easy trails for snowmobiles. Parts of the park are open to automobiles during winter, making this option an easy one. A popular trail I highly recommend, is the scenic ride to the summit of **Signal Mountain**. Reach the trail from the north entrance of the park, just down the road from the Signal Mountain Lodge. Continue south on the unplowed section of the road another mile, then turn left to begin your 4-mile ascent to the summit. This trail is also popular with cross-country skiers.

There are a number of snowmobile rental businesses and guided tour operators in Jackson Hole. They offer guided excursions or only supply the machine and snowsuit thereby allowing you to customize your own riding experience. Weekends book-up early, so reserve ahead or plan your trip mid-week instead. Rates range from $75 - $125 per snowmachine and Visa, Mastercard and American Express are generally accepted.

The following businesses rent snowmachines and snowsuits for the Jackson Hole area and can provide you with maps of snowmobile trails and other pertinent information. For information about rental companies in other gateway towns such as Gardiner, Cody or West Yellowstone, contact the local chambers of commerce for that area.

►**Yellowstone Snowmobile Tours: (307) 733-5863**
►**National Parks Adventures: (307) 733-1572**
►**Jackson Hole Snowmobile: (307) 739-9477**
►**Leisure Sports: (307) 733:3040**
►**Flagg Ranch Village: (307) 733-3040**
►**Wyoming Adventures: (307) 733-2300**

Bicycling and Mountain Biking

Beyond a doubt, you have entered one of the bicycling meccas of the west! Bicycling and mountain biking are both popular in Jackson Hole and there are endless miles of challenging trails just about everywhere in the valley.

On any given day, in any area, you're likely to encounter these fat-tired bikes on any trail open to them.

Bicycles are not permitted on trails in the national parks, (they are permitted along the roadways, anywhere an automobile can legally travel) but trails that do permit bikes are as numerous as they are varied. Any of the following bike rental companies can provide free maps of local bike routes.

For those wanting to bike near the town of Jackson, the **Cache Creek-Game Creek Trail** is a "must do." The trail begins southeast of town, at Cache Creek Drive. The trail climbs steadily to the Cache Creek trail and Game Creek turnoff, then crosses Cache Creek. For its scenic descent, the trail narrows to a single track. Once at the bottom, a short ride north along the roadway leads you back into town. The ride take between 3-4 hours.

To rent your own bicycle for a day or a week, contact any of these bicycle specialists:

▸**Mountain Bike Outfitters: (307) 733-3314**
Moose, near entrance to Teton National Park
▸**Teton Cyclery: (307) 733-4386**
175 N. Glenwood St.
▸**Leisure Sports: (307) 733-3040**
1075 S. U.S. Highway 89
▸**Hoback Sports: (307) 733-5335**
40 S. Millward St.

HELICOPTER, AIRPLANE, GLIDER RIDES

For a unique experience during your stay in the valley, various companies offer aerial tours of Yellowstone, Teton and the valley.

If you are a powder hound and seek vast, remote miles of untracked snow, you should consider the ultimate ski adventure; helicopter skiing. On otherwise inaccessible snowy ranges such as the Tetons, Hobacks, Palisades and the Snake River, you'll find varied terrain offering everything from tree and glade skiing to open-bowl skiing.

For more information about "getting off the ground," contact the following companies:

►**High Mountains Helicopter Skiing**, located in Jackson, services intermediate to expert rated ski runs. A day of skiing consists of 13,000 to 15,000 vertical feet of untracked lines. For more information, call 733-3274.

►**Jackson Hole Aviation,** located at the airport, offers scenic flights of the valley. Call 733-4767.

►**Mountain Rotors, Inc.,** offers tours of Yellowstone and Teton National Parks. Call 733-1633.

►**Grand Valley Aviation,** located in Driggs, Idaho, offers glider rides in the Tetons. Call (208) 354-8131.

151

WATER, WATER, EVERYWHERE

FISHING

Anglers throughout the world are attracted to the incredible trout fishing this region offers. There are few places on earth that blends incredible scenery with unparalleled trout fishing. For fishing in Jackson Hole in May and June, your best bet for catching lake trout, would be spin casting from the area's larger lakes. In July, when streams begin to run clear, you'll find an abundance of cutthroat trout in the area's rivers and streams.

One of the most popular destinations in Jackson Hole is the Snake River. For fly rods and spinners, an exceptionally good spot is just below **Jackson Lake Dam**. Another popular spot is just southwest of Jackson, in the **Snake River Canyon**. Southeast of Jackson, you'll find the **Hoback River**, a tributary of the Snake, to be another easily accessed spot for cutthroat trout.

The most popular fishing regions in Yellowstone National Park is the **Yellowstone, Firehole** and **Madison Rivers**. A variety of native and non-native trout can be

152

found here, and a multitude of regulations along with them.

With so many anglers wanting to test their skill, it's easy to understand why fishing is strictly regulated. All persons twelve or older must possess a valid permit to fish in Yellowstone. Permits are available free from any ranger station, visitor center or Hamilton store throughout the park. In most regions of the park, fishing season lasts from Memorial Day through October. While the park does try to provide the visitor with fishing enjoyment, it is stressed that this resource is an important part of the natural system. Fish are a critical food source for grizzly bears, pelicans, osprey and bald eagles. The "catch and return" policy is highly encouraged while fishing the lakes and streams of Yellowstone.

Teton National Park requires a valid Wyoming fishing license. Pay special attention to regulations while fishing in Teton. Special rules may apply for catching and releasing spawn-size fish.

For more information on where to find the best fish-activity, to rent equipment for your fishing needs or to plan a guided fishing trip, contact any of the following companies:

▸**Jack Dennis Sports,** located on the south side of the Town Square, 485 W. Broadway. Offers rental equipment, up-to-date fishing information and a large selection of fly-fishing gear. Call 733-3270.

▸**Orvis,** located at 485 W. Broadway, offers fishing gear and provides guided fishing trips. Call 733-5407.

▸**Signal Mountain Lodge,** located in Grand Teton National Park on Jackson Lake, offers equipment and guided lake and river fishing trips. Call 733-5470.

▸**Westbank Anglers,** located on Teton Village Road, is a full service fly shop and offers guided fly-fishing trips. Call 733-6483.

CANOEING, BOATING AND RAFTING

If you're looking to get wet and wild during your stay in Jackson Hole, you won't be disappointed. There are many rivers and lakes in the valley and the national parks, all surrounded by breathtaking scenery. The waters in this region will offer you everything from a languid scenic canoe trip to a white-knuckled, bone rattling white water experience you'll never forget.

There are six lakes in Grand Teton National Park offering a variety of boating options. Boaters within Teton will need to purchase a permit. The fee is $10 for a motorized vessel and $5.00 for nonmotorized. You can use this permit for Yellowstone National Park as well. **Water-skiing, windsurfing** and **sailing** is allowed on Jackson Lake. The **Oxbow bend** area is an excellent spot for the leisure canoeist and provides prime opportunity for spotting wildlife and waterfowl. **String and Leigh Lakes** offer placid paddling as well. The shallow waters of String Lake provide a rare opportunity for swimming, unlike the park's larger lakes, which are much too frigid for even the hardiest of swimmers.

While the waters of Yellowstone have more restrictive boating regulations, there are a variety canoeing and boating opportunities available. **Bridge Bay Marina** operates scenic boat tours of **Yellowstone Lake** ($6.00 for adults and $3.00 for children) and rents motorboats ($15-$20 per hour). A rowboat can be had for as little as $3.50 per hour. If you bring your own motorboat, bear in mind that motorboats are only permitted on parts of Yellowstone and Lewis Lakes. All vessels are prohibited on park rivers and streams with the exception of the channel between Lewis and Shoshone Lakes, which only allows hand-propelled vessels. You will need to obtain a boating permit available at the Lake Ranger station or Grant Village Visitor Center. The fee is $10 for a motorized vessel and $5.00 for nonmotorized. You can use this permit for Grand Teton National Park as well.

The Snake River provides a wide range of canoeing, floating, kayaking and rafting options to accommodate the novice and well as the expert. For the more adventurous types who want to test their nerve, **whitewater rafting** will get their blood boiling. One of the most popular white-water runs includes the shoot through the raging rapids of the Snake River Canyon. These trips last between 3-4 hours and cost $15-$25 for adults and $15-$20 for children. Be prepared to get wet and leave your camera at home.

For those who desire a more gentle river experience, try **floating**. There are several sections of the Snake, the most popular being between Jackson Lake Dam and Pacific Creek, that are tame enough even for the most novice floaters. After this point, conditions take on a considerably wilder feel. Expect to pay $15-$25 for adults and $10-$15 for children for guided float trips. Rountrip transportation is usually provided by most companies.

Before beginning your boat excursion, check in with the Bridger-Teton National Forest office in Jackson, (307) 733-2752. They will be able to provide you with the most up-to-date boating regulations and river conditions. Grand Teton National Park provides a helpful brochure on running the park portions of the Snake. The brochure is called *Floating the Snake* and is free.

Even boaters experienced with floating the Snake should always check river conditions before starting out. River conditions change on a daily basis. Water depths can vary widely, spring flows can be very high and constantly shifting logjams can make for unpredictable and hazardous conditions.

Call any of the following companies for information and rentals. Expect to pay around $25 per day for canoes, $40 per day for kayaks and $50 per day for floats. Paddles, life jackets and roof racks are included. Some of these companies provide guided excursions, overnight trips and instructional classes.

►**WHITEWATER TRIPS**
Barker-Ewing Whitewater: (307) 733-1000
Dave Hanson Whitewater: (307) 733-6295
Jackson Hole Whitewater: (307) 733-1007
Lewis and Clark Expeditions: (307) 733-4022
Mad River Boat Trips: (307) 733-6203
Sands' Wildwater: (307) 733-4410
Snake River Park Whitewater: (307) 733-7078

►**FLOATING**
Barker Ewing: (307) 733-1800
Barlow River Trips: (307) 733-9392
Flagg Ranch: (307) 733-8761
Grand Teton Lodge Company: (307) 733-2811

Lewis and Clark Expeditions: (307) 733-4022
Signal Mountain Lodge: (307) 733-5470
Solitude Float Trips: (307) 733-2871

▶**BOAT AND CANOE RENTALS**
Bridge Bay Marina (Yellowstone):
Hungry Jack's: (307) 733-3561
Leisure Sports: (307) 733-3040

▶**WINDSURFING**
Alpine Windsurfing: (307) 733-4460

JACKSON HOLE, WYOMING

INTRODUCTION
JACKSON, WYOMING

T he town of Jackson (pop. 5,200) is located at the southern end of Jackson Hole and is nestled between mountains on three sides; Snow King Mountain, the East Gros Ventre and the Gros Ventre Range. Though no one will dispute the greatest appeal to the valley of Jackson Hole is the exquisite sights, sounds and experiences to be found in the great outdoors, many visitors are surprised to learn of the many events and attractions that are available in the small town of Jackson.

First time visitors to Jackson are guaranteed to be charmed by its western-style and laid-back ways. At the heart of Jackson is the Town Square, a postcard-perfect little park decked with its famous elk antler arches at its four corners. You could wile away many an hour here, watching the youth play hackey-sack or simply taking in the riot of golden autumn leaves on the cottonwoods and aspens. Reebok and Docker clad tourists and local teenagers sporting mohawks and rollerblades mingle on the wooden sidewalks of the square in strange harmony. If you're observant, you may even see a famous person or two: actors Harrison Ford, Ed Asner and former Secretary of the Interior, James

Watt and members of the Rockefeller family maintain, at least part-time, residences here.

The wooden sidewalks of Jackson, its weekly rodeos, log cabins, covered wagon trips, chuckwagon dinner shows and working dude ranches all signify the town's desire to hold true to its natural history. This remarkable achievement, combined with the areas intimate scale and leisurely pace have made Jackson more than just a stop-over to the bounty of parks and ski areas. The town itself has developed (to the dismay of locals and visitors alike) into a first class resort - a destination in itself. Nearly three million people will pass through this area each year and the tiny town of Jackson has had to make major adjustments to handle the crush of visitors. They have succeeded. The square is packed with art galleries, museums, restaurants, theaters, boutiques and just about everything else imaginable! Lodging, shopping, restaurants, entertainment and public transportation are all generally excellent throughout the valley.

Choosing to forgo the polish and glitter of other more "posh" resorts, Jackson struggles, amid rapid growth, to remain a *real* western town. They have *nearly* succeeded. Along with the authentic western you'll also find the pseudo-western: Stores with false-facades stocking the usual tourist paraphernalia: everything from rubber tomahawks and moose-antlered hats to

161

instructional book on how to talk like a "real cowboy." Yes, commercial industry is booming here in Jackson and you don't have to look too far to evidence this. K-mart and Pizza Hut both occupy old ranch lands and several scenic country roads are slated for widening. Downtown merchants are counting their days before the development of a new mall begins less than 2 miles from the Town Square. The small local population laments that housing has become unaffordable and many have had to move to more affordable communities such as nearby Driggs and Afton. (In 1989 Teton Village land prices rose a staggering 100%!) Certainly the same problems that plague other resorts like Aspen or Vail, exist here as well. Formed specifically to address these issues, **The Jackson Hole Alliance for Responsible Planning** and **The Jackson Hole Land Trust** are working to protect and preserve the community and the natural areas of Jackson Hole for future generations.

For now, the beauty and western traditions that work together to make Jackson great are still here. Known as the Last of the Wild West, let's hope it remains that way.

VISITOR INFORMATION

TIME: All of Wyoming is on Mountain Standard Time or Mountain Daylight Time.

ELEVATION: The valley floor is at an elevation between 6,200 and 6,800 feet above sea level. The top of the Grand Teton is at 13,770 feet.

LOCATION: Located in the northwestern corner of Wyoming, Jackson Hole is a 60 mile long, 20 mile wide alpine valley, bordered by the Teton Mountain Range on the west and girded by the Gros Ventre Mountains on the east.

POPULATION: The population of the entire county (or valley) is approximately 13,150, while the population of the city of Jackson is 5,200.

CLIMATE:

Average Temperatures

	HIGH	LOW		HIGH	LOW
January	28°	2°	July	79°	41°
February	33°	7°	August	78°	37°
March	38°	13°	September	69°	32°
April	48°	22°	October	54°	22°
May	59°	31°	November	39°	14°
June	68°	37°	December	26°	6°

THE JACKSON HOLE CHAMBER OF COMMERCE: Located at 532 N. Cache, just 5 blocks from the Town Square. Operates the Wyoming Travel Center in Jackson Hole and is open year round. Hours are as follows:

June 15 - Labor Day: 7 days a week from 8 a.m.- 8 p.m.

Sept.15 - Oct. 15: 7 days a week 8 a.m. - 5 p.m.

Oct. 15 - May 15: 7 days a week Mon.- Fri. 8 a.m.-5 p.m., Sat.-Sun 10 a.m.-2 p.m..

May 15 - June 15: 7 days a week 8 a.m. - 5 p.m.

MEETINGS AND CONVENTIONS: The Chamber of Commerce has a complete listing of all conference locations and a description of the facilities.

TRANSPORTATION:

By Air

Jackson Hole is serviced directly by air via Denver, Chicago, Salt Lake City and Dallas/Fortworth by three major airlines: American Airlines, Delta Airlines and United Express Airlines.

Local Transportation

Jackson Hole Transportation shuttles meet every incoming flight with drop-off points between Jackson and Teton Village and will also provide drop-off for departures. Many lodging facilities offer free airport shuttles for their guests. Taxi service, charter and rental cars are also available.

Jackson Hole Transportation 733-3135
A-1 Taxi   733-5089
Access Tours (able/disable) 733-6664
Buckboard Cab   733-1112
Tumbleweed Taxi   733-0808

RENTAL CARS:
Avis   733-3422 or (800) 343-2755
Budget   733-2206 or (800) 527-0700
Dollar Saver 733-2222
Hertz   733-2272 or (800) 654-3131
Jackson Hole 733-6868 or (800) 722-2002
National   733-4132 or (800) CAR-RENT
Rent-A-Wreck 733-5014
Resort   733-1656 or (800) 289-3538
Teton Motors 733-6600

High Altitude Medical Tips:
While most people who come to Jackson Hole will not experience any medical problems, the following information may answer any questions you may have about altitude related illnesses.

Acute Mountain Sickness
Acute Mountain Sickness, also known as AMS, is a condition that can range from a mild headache to incapacitation. About 5% of Jackson Hole's visitors will

experience a mild form of AMS. This generally occurs when one sleeps at altitudes above 8,000 feet. Since the valley floor sits at an elevation of approximately 6,200 feet, this rarely poses a serious threat to most visitors. Frequent symptoms include headache, nausea, insomnia, lack of appetite, fatigue and lightheadedness. Bed rest coupled with plenty of fluids will improve these conditions within 24 to 48 hours.

Dehydration

Since relative humidity is very low in Jackson Hole, dehydration occurs here much more frequently than at lower elevations. A good rule of thumb for determining how much fluid is enough to prevent dehydration, is to drink enough to cause the need for urination at least every 3 hours. *Always* take a water bottle for vigorous hikes or other such activities. Symptoms include headache and fatigue.

Sunburn

Sunblock is mandatory in winter as well as summer. High altitude means less atmosphere to filter out harmful ultraviolet rays which could result in a painful burn or snow blindness. Snow blindness can be prevented by wearing UV filtered sunglasses.

Frostbite

Frostbite occurs when your skin and the underlying tissue have actually begun to freeze. The areas most often affected are the smaller extremities: fingers, toes, nose and cheeks. The affected areas initially turn white then red and will hurt during rewarming. You should seek medical attention if you think you are experiencing frostbite.

Nosebleeds

Because of the low humidity in Jackson Hole, nosebleeds may occur more frequently, especially during the early morning hours. Some hotels provide a room humidifier, which should help to alleviate this problem.

Alcohol

The affects of drugs and alcohol are doubled at increased altitudes. Which, by the way, means that your hangovers will also be worse.

Hospital - Medical Help

Should you have any other medical questions or need medical service, contact St. Johns Hospital or Emerg+A+Care at the following locations:

► **St. John's Hospital** provides a free patient shuttle 8-5 daily and can be reached by calling 733-3636, 24 hours

167

a day or for emergencies you may dial 911. They are located at 625 Broadway, about 1 mile east of the Town Square.

▶**Emerg+A+Care** is located in the Powderhorn Mall on N. Broadway. St. at 733-8002. They are open 7 days a week with office hours from 9-7 and emergencies 24 hours a day.

Church Services
Church services of various denominations are located throughout Jackson.
Christian Science Society
Cache and Gill. 733-4744
Church of Christ
174 N. King
733-2611
Church of Jesus Christ,
Latter Day Saints, 1st. Ward
512 E. Broadway
733-5657
First Baptist Church
Glenwood and Kelly. 733-3706
St. John's Episcopal Church
Glenwood and Gill. 733-2603
Our Lady of the Mountains Catholic Church
201 S. Jackson St. 733-7745

Annual Events

Spring

Perhaps the world's only public **elk antler auction** is held on the Town's Square in late May. This event lures hundreds of travelers from all over the world, eager to bid on the nearly 3 tons of antlers collected from the nearby National Elk Refuge by local Boy Scouts. The antlers are shed naturally by the elk each winter and are used in the making of furniture or ground to powder to be used for Oriental love potions for the South Korean and Chinese markets. Antlers sell for as much as $14.00 per pound, with the proceeds being used to help feed the elk that winter on the refuge.

Summer

Kick off your Memorial Day weekend with **Old West Days,** a western theme celebration complete with parades, rodeos, Indian dancing, a mountain man rendezvous and more. If you're planning a trip to Jackson to celebrate Independence Day, you should book early. This is a favorite among locals and visitors alike. Parades, special rodeos and barbecues all precede a dazzling fireworks display, beginning at dusk at the base of Snow King Mountain. The **Grand Teton Music Festival,** located at Teton Village, performs classical and modern works. (See page 179 for details.)

Summer nights (Wednesdays and Saturdays) are reserved for those hard-riding, bronco-bustin cowboys at the **Jackson Rodeo**, located at the Teton County Fair Grounds. Don't miss one of these spectacular shows. Kids get to join in the fun and feel like real cowboys and cowgirls during the kiddie calf-scramble.

For intellectual stimulation, attend one of the many science and nature seminars at **The Science School.** Workshops are held throughout the summer. In late July, head down to the Jackson Hole Rodeo Grounds for the always-exciting **Teton County Fair.** Usually slated for July or August, **The Mountain Artists Rendezvous**, is a large arts and crafts fair held each year on the lawn of St. John's Church.

Fall

Autumn is spectacular in Jackson Hole. The cottonwoods and aspens are a shimmer of gold against the Tetons. Tourists have flocked back to their far corners leaving the valley to the hardier travelers and locals to experience its cool, quiet beauty. The **Jackson Hole Fall Arts Festival** is the major fall event, featuring exhibits by local artists and galleries, theater productions, dance performances, concerts, poetry readings and more.

Winter

The **Torchlight Ski Parades** take place on Christmas Eve and New Year's Eve, beginning at dusk at all three ski resorts. Choose to watch or join in the fun. **Ski race** events go on all winter, ending with the annual **Pole-Pedal-Paddle-Race**. This is a wild and sometimes grueling competition, combining alpine and cross-country skiing, cycling and canoeing. The very fit need only apply! The local Shriners hold their annual **Cutter Races** during the months of January and February. What exactly is a cutter race? Imagine a hair-raisingly-wild horse and chariot, careening across a sheet of frozen ice about a quarter of a mile long. Sound exciting enough for you? Located at Melody Ranch, about six miles south of Jackson.

For more information about annual events in Jackson, call 307-733-3316 or visit the Information Center on North Cache.

AREA ATTRACTIONS

Tourist Information

First time visitors should be sure to visit the **Wyoming State Information Center**, located at 532 N. Cache. Hours are daily 8:00 a.m. to 8:00 p.m. mid-June through Labor Day and 8:30 to 5:30 Monday through Friday and Sunday, 10:00 to 2:00 the rest of the year. The center has a wealth of free information and maps to the areas attractions and services. You'll also find direct phone lines to dozens of local hotels and motels. Be sure to pick up a free copy of **The Jackson Hole Dining Guide**. It lists the more than 70 restaurants you have to choose from during your stay in the valley.

Be sure to look for the steps that lead upstairs to the observation deck. This will afford you a nice overview of The National Elk Refuge.

To request free maps and brochures before coming to Jackson Hole, call The Jackson Hole's Visitors Council, telephone: 1-800-782-0011.

Art Galleries

Upon first glance, most first time visitors to Jackson Hole may make the mistake of assuming that all the spectacular scenery can only be found in the great outdoors. What may surprise you however, is the abundance of wildlife and western landscape scenes you'll discover in the many galleries and museums that line the streets of the Town Square. While Jackson Hole may not have the appearance of a nationally ranked art market, Jackson has, within the past decade, taken its place along side Santa Fe, NM and Scottsdale, AZ, as one of the major art centers for Western Art in the United States. Like any area, the variety and quality of artwork runs the spectrum. You will find everything from high quality photographic exhibits and exquisite Indian antiquities to pastel Southwestern-style pottery and mass-produced prints of coyotes howling at the moon.

The secret to Jackson's cultural success lies all around you. The valley and its surroundings are an artists dream. Wildlife and landscape artists such as Charles Russell and Conrad Schwiering have built their entire careers trying to express the excitement the spectacular forests, mountains and wildlife of this region created in them. So take in a photo exhibit to see the works of Ansel Adams or browse through the collection of Fredric Remington paintings. The spirit and mystery of the land will remain with you forever. Who knows...you may be inspired to sign up for a course in photography or watercolor!

The following is a list of recommended galleries and museums.

▸**BIG HORN GALLERY,** located on the Town Square, specializes in western and wildlife paintings and sculptures. Located upstairs at 98 Center Street, above Buffalo Trail Gallery. For more information call 733-1434.

▸**CENTER STREET GALLERY,** features Southwestern and contemporary art by such notables as Frank Howell, R. C. Gorman, Pablo Antonio Milan, Katalin Ehling, Bill Worrell and Dan Hemann. The Center Street Gallery is located at 172 Center Street. For more information call (307) 733-1115.

▸**GALLERY OF THE WEST,** offers a magnificent selection of bronzes and sculptures of eagles, Indians, cowboys and wildlife. You have two locations to choose from: upstairs in Chet's Way near the square and at 110 East Broadway.

▸**JACK DENNIS' WYOMING GALLERIES,** displays an extensive collection of original wildlife, sporting art and limited edition prints. Located above the Jack Dennis' Outdoor Shop on the Town Square. Newsletters and catalog are available by calling (800) 522-5755.

▸**RAWSON GALLERIES,** features contemporary artwork by notable Phil Clark, avant garde artists Makaaki Noda and Kenjilo Nanao and watercolors and etchings in a more traditional vein by Tom Ketron, Christie Kemp and Sheila Langlois. Rawson Galleries is located on King Street, across from the Sweetwater Restaurant.

▸**TRAILSIDE GALLERIES,** offers a fine collection of artwork ranging from Western realism, traditional wildlife and landscapes, to American Impressionism. Trailside Galleries represents over 90 artists, including the works of Joe Beeler, Fred Fellows, Harvey Johnson, Bill Nebecker, Jim Norton and Bill Moyers. You'll also find the work of past masters such as John Clymer, Charlie Dye, Charles Russell and Fredric Remington. Located on the north side of the Town Square. (307) 733-3186.

MUSEUMS

WILDLIFE OF THE AMERICAN WEST ART MUSEUM, located on the northeast corner of the Jackson Town Square, houses the country's premier public collection of North American Wildlife Art. More than 250 sculptures, bronzes, and wildlife paintings are featured here, making it the largest such collection in the world. At the core of the collection is a selection of oil paintings, sculptures, dry points and watercolors by the master in the field of big game animals; Carl Rungius. Other prominent painters and sculptors include George Catlin, Albert Bierstadt, Charles M. Russell and local artists Clymer and

175

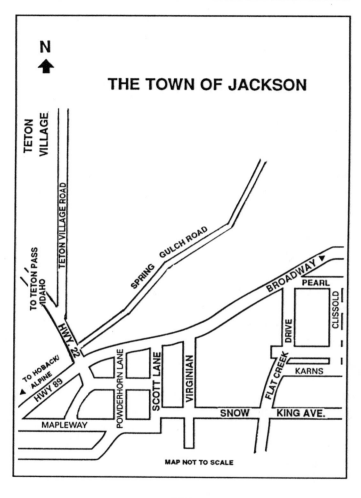

N

THE TOWN OF JACKSON

TETON VILLAGE

TETON VILLAGE ROAD

TO TETON PASS
IDAHO

SPRING GULCH ROAD

BROADWAY ▼

PEARL

CLISSOLD

HWY 22

TO HOBACK/
ALPINE ▲

HWY 89

POWDERHORN LANE

SCOTT LANE

VIRGINIAN

FLAT CREEK DRIVE

KARNS

MAPLEWAY

SNOW

KING AVE.

MAP NOT TO SCALE

176

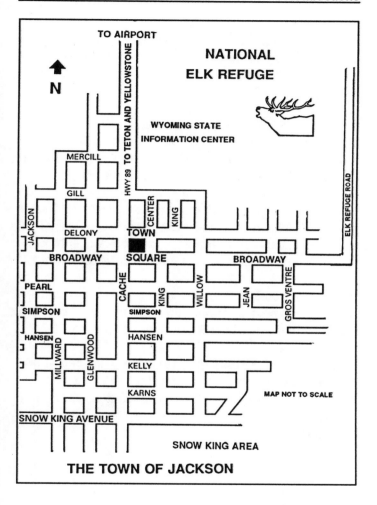

THE TOWN OF JACKSON

Schwiering. Admission is $2, or $5 per family. Open during the summer months from 1-6 on Sundays, Mon.-thru Sat. 10-6. Winter hours are Sun. 1-5 and Tues.-Sat. 10-5.

THE JACKSON HOLE MUSEUM, located at 105 N. Glenwood and the **TETON COUNTY HISTORICAL CENTER**, located at 105 Mercill, display exhibits on Jackson Hole's settlement history from the days of trappers, Indians, cattlemen and dude ranchers. A replica of the "Colter Stone" is on display at the Historical Center along with a interesting collection of photos and historical archives. Admission to the Jackson Hole Museum is $2 for adults and $5 for families. Summer hours are from 10-4 on Sundays and 9-6 Monday-Saturday. Admission to the Teton County Historical Center is free; hours are Monday-Friday 1-5 during the summer months and Monday-Friday 1-5 from September - May.

THE WILDLIFE MUSEUM & Taxidermy, located at 862 W. Broadway, displays menacing stuffed bears and all the other wildlife indigenous to this area. It is particularly popular with the kids. Admission is $2 for adults and $1 for children.

The Grand Teton Music Festival

The rustic qualities of Wyoming do not lend themselves easily to the idea of world-class musical talents performing full-orchestra concerts, solo-performances and piano recitals in the shadow of the craggy Tetons. But lend themselves they do - for more than 30 harmonious years now. The Grand Teton Music Festival represents more than 200 professional musicians, one hundred student musicians and of course one talented director- Maestro Ling Tung. Maestro Tung has an exalted reputation for his dedication to the highest standards of performance. He has appeared and recorded with London's Philharmonia Orchestra and has also conducted the Royal Philharmonic, the Vienna Symphony, and the Radio Orchestras of Hamburg, Stuttgart and Berlin. In America, Maestro Tung has conducted the New York Philharmonic and the Symphony Orchestras of Milwaukee, Pittsburgh, Honolulu, New Orleans, and Utah.

Beginning in June, concerts are held six nights a week in Walk Festival Hall, a theater with better acoustics than most of New York City's best halls. The theater's seven hundred seats tend to sell out early due to the heavy concentration of visitors summering in the valley - so please reserve early.

Ticket prices range from $5.00 to $15.00, with student discounts available. For more information call **(307) 733-3050.**

Live Musical Theaters

Summers in Jackson Hole offer a variety of live, western-theme theater and broadway shows for the entire family. Among these are **Dirty Jack's Wild West Theater,** located at 140 N. Cache (733-4775), **Jackson Hole Playhouse**, located at 145 W. Deloney (733-6994 and the **Pink Garter Theater**, located at 49 W. Broadway, (733-6994).

Tram Ride

One of the best ways to get a bird's eye view of Jackson Hole is to hitch a ride on the Aerial Tram to the top of Rendezvous Peak, more than 10,000 feet above sea level. The tram takes about 12 minutes to reach the summit and once on top you'll be rewarded with one of the most arresting vistas ever observed. The high rugged peaks, distant valleys and the winding Snake River provides the observer with a view some consider to be the most impressive in all of North America. These mountain peaks are just babies as far a mountains go: only 10 million years old, while the Rockies are at least 50 million years old. The true elders however, are the Appalachians, which are dated somewhere near 200 million years old.

Choose one of the several nature trails and take a walk along the mountain's summit. The Summit Nature

Loop is a short self-guided walk around Rendezvous Peak. The Cody Bowl Trail and Rock Springs Trail are both rated moderate in difficulty (I suggest a pair of sturdy hiking shoes) and will take anywhere from 2-4 hours to return to the tram. For quick refreshments, a small snack bar is located near the tram entrance.

If you choose to hike back down, the Mountain Road Trail would be the easiest route and is 7.2 miles in length. This is not actually a trail but a wide service road which is rocky and very steep in certain areas. It's a long, but interesting hike and should you decide to go for it, take a few precautions: take along a water bottle, be sure to bring a sweater or rain gear because of the cooler climate at this elevation and make sure to wear comfortable footwear. The day I hiked this trail, I encountered several grazing moose with calf and a pair of porcupines engaged in what appeared to be a rather tricky mating game. Other wildlife more commonly found are the golden mantled ground squirrel, snowshoe hare and the red fox. The Audubon Society has counted more than 80 different species of birds here, including eagles, ravens, cliff swallows, and mountain bluebirds.

Ticket prices are as follows:

Adults:	$13.00
Seniors:	$11.00
Children 13-18:	6.00
Children 6-12:	2.00

Children under five are free.

Hours vary with each season, so be sure to check the schedule at the ticket office located in the clock tower at Teton Village, or call (307) 733-2292.

Snow King Chair Lift

For a less expensive view of the valley, though certainly still spectacular, take the chairlift to the top of Snow King Mountain. At an elevation of nearly 8,000 feet, the panorama includes five different mountain ranges. Take a walk along the short nature trail along the ridge. During the spring the mountain is ablaze with duncecap larkstrums and a host of other wildflowers. There is a picnic area on the summit. Ticket prices are $6.00 for adults and $2 for children under 12. (307) 733-5200.

National Elk Refuge

Located approximately 3 miles north of Jackson, the National Elk Refuge supports nearly 10,000 elk each winter. During the summer months, elk prefer the high country of the north and east of Jackson Hole. But when the snow falls, these regal animals descend from their lofty elevations and remain on the elk refuge and the surrounding valley until spring. This 25,000 acre plot holds one of the two largest native elk herds in the United States. Thousands of elk can be seen from the highway as one travels U.S. 89 on the western edge of the refuge.

The elk, also known as Wapiti by the Shoshone Indians, have wintered in this valley since prehistoric times. But as the valley became settled, by the late 1800's, the elk's migratory route became fenced by early ranchers for the containment of livestock. The elk could no longer reach their winter food and thousands of elk died each year as a result.

In an effort to save the starving elk, local rancher Stephen Leek photographed the thousands of dead and starving elk and used the photos to pressure the State of Wyoming to appropriate funds for feeding the animals. In 1909, the state purchased $5,000 in hay to feed the starving elk. Two years later, the federal government began buying land for the refuge and by 1913 the National Elk Refuge was established. The elk herd is fed nearly 30 tons of pelleted alfalfa **each day**, partly paid for by the sale of elk antlers auctioned off on the Town Square each spring.

One of the highlights of a winter trip to Jackson Hole is visiting the refuge. Each year, the public is offered the unique opportunity to observe and photograph these majestic animals from a close-up perspective. Horse-drawn sleighs carry you silently into the wintering herd of 7,000 to 10,000 elk. Definitely, another Kodak moment. Rides last for 30-45 minutes and cost $6.00 for adults and $3.00 for children.

The **Elk Refuge Visitor Center**, tele: 733-9212, provides information and books about the elk herd and the refuge. This is also where you will wait for the horse-drawn sleigh ride. The sleighs run daily from 10-4 from late December to late March.

Granite Hot Springs

Granite Hot Springs is a little off the beaten path, but the drive is a scenic and pleasurable one. Bring your bathing suit for a relaxing soak in a natural hot springs pool (105°) amidst rugged canyon walls. This is also a popular snowmobile destination in the winter. Since the dirt road remains unplowed during the winter months, snowmobilers have this region to themselves. Just wear your bathing suit under your ski-suit and go for it! Warming huts, fortunately, are available. There is a snack bar on the premises and admission is $4 for adults and $2 for children. Located approximately 35 miles North from the Town Square, take 89 N to Hoback Junction then turn left towards Pinedale. You will pass through rugged canyons along the winding Hoback River until you reach the junction of Granite Hot Springs Road. This is where Granite Creek merges with the Hoback River. Turn left. You will take a dirt road (hopefully it will be recently graded) another 10 miles to the springs.

Golf and Tennis

For those who begin to yearn for more urbane activities while visiting the valley, you can visit one of Jackson's two first class golf and tennis centers.

Jackson Hole Golf and Tennis

Located minutes north of Jackson off route 89, is an 18 hole par, 72 championship golf course. 110 yards of fairways and greens, bordered by Grand Teton National Park. Also provided is a swimming pool and six tennis courts. All facilities are open to the public, and several membership options are offered. **733-7788.**

Teton Pines Golf and Tennis

Located on Teton Village Road. This Arnold Palmer designed course offers a 17 par and 17,400 yard course at the foot of the Tetons. Teton Pines also sports the **Teton Pines Tennis Pavilion**; a tennis center offering 7 courts, three of which are operable during the winter under an inflatable dome. All facilities are open to the public, with several membership options available. **733-9248.**

Jackson Rodeo

Rodeo action is one of the communities most impressive and popular attractions. The rodeo begins at 8:00 every Wednesday and Saturday night from Memorial Day to Labor Day. Cowboys and cowgirls come from all around the region to jockey for position as top in their field. Competition includes barrel racing, roping events, steer wrestling, bull riders and the most exciting of all; the bucking bronco riders. Children get to join in the fun during the kiddie calf scramble - another Kodak moment!

Single adult admission is $6.50 and the price for children under 12 is $4.00. A family rate is available for $21.00. Located at the Teton County Fairgrounds. For more information call **733-2806.**

The Cowboy Shootout

During the summer months, the streets downtown are closed to traffic while costumed, local performers reenact all the lawlessness of the wild west days, staging western shoot-outs and hangings on the Town Square. Spectators are often encouraged to participate and the show is free. Begins at 6.00 p.m. Mon-Fri. each evening daily.

The Alpine Slide

For those with young ones in their party, (or the very young at heart) visit the Alpine Slide, located at the base of Snow King Mountain. The slide winds down 2,500 feet of treed mountainside. You control your own speed, and no special skill is required. Look for the yellow and blue chairlift located directly above the Snow King Resort Hotel. Snack bar available. Ticket prices are $4 and $3 for children under 12. Tele: 733-7680.

SHOPPING

There are a few things you won't find in Jackson Hole. For instance you won't find a very good selection of haute couture and we don't have any Rolls Royce dealerships. Other than that, you'll find just about anything else you might be looking for. Most of Jackson Hole's shopping is centered around the Town Square area, although some shops can be found along Highway 89 within a mile or two of the square. Just like in any other city you should shop around for the best price. Don't buy the very first navajo rug, oil painting or ski jacket that catches your eye; check to see if it is available at another shop at a less expensive price.

Prices for clothing in Jackson Hole seems to be a bit pricier that you'd normally find in other areas, however the quality does seem to be quite good in most shops. Factory outlet stores such as Ralph Lauren Polo, J. Crew, Benetton, Fila and London Fog all offer items priced from slightly to significantly below average retail. Of special interest to shoppers in Jackson are the myriad

187

of shops offering attractive selections of western clothing, western boots, belts and hats, leather goods, handmade jewelry and western and Indian pottery and artwork all ranging in quality anywhere from sublime to kitschy. Listed below, you'll find a range of shopping experiences to suit every taste and budget.

Hide Out Leather and Fine Apparel: Supremely soft and unique leather and suede jackets, boots, bags, clothing and accessories. Located at 40 Center St. **733-2422.**

Jackson Hole Ski and Sports: One of the largest collections of outdoor gear including mountain bikes, ski sales and rentals, hiking and camping equipment, and designer name footwear and sportswear such as Bogner, Tecnica, Nils, Rossignol, Nordica and more. Located at 455 West Broadway. **733-4449.**

The "Hole" Works: Interesting gifts, Indian jewelry, animal skins, beads and a good selection of western and Indian reading. Located upstairs in the Cache Creek Mall on the Town Square. **733-7000.**

Valley Book Store: This is the place to pick up beautiful photographic art books of the mountains, wildlife and plantlife indigenous to Wyoming and the Rockies or catch up on the latest Stephen King or John Updike novel. Located in Gaslight Alley on the Town Square. **733-4533.**

Teton Book Shop: Carries a variety of books and magazines. Local interest reading material, maps and greeting cards are also available. 25 S. Glenwood. **733-9220.**

The Mangy Moose Mall: Located in Teton Village and houses **The Rocky Mountain Chocolate Factory, Sirk Shirts, Snake River Trading Company** and **The Mangy Moose Gift Shop**. 733-4913.

Two Grey Hills: Interesting selection of Navajo weavings, Indian jewelry, pottery, baskets and Hopi Kachinas. Located at the corner of Broadway and King. **733-2677.**

Baggits: An interesting boutique packed with the newest ladies western wear, sportswear and accessories. Baggits is located at 35 West Broadway. **733-1234**.

Wyoming Woolens: Good quality warm clothing and outerwear made locally. Wyoming Woolens has two locations to choose from: a retail shop located at 20 W. Broadway, and a factory outlet, where you will find much better buys, at 870 S Hwy. 89. **733-2991**.

The County Parks and Recreation Department: Loans free tents, sleeping bags and recreational equipment with a $50.00 deposit. These supplies are not exactly *new* - but they are free. Located at 181 S. King St. **733-5056.**

Jack Dennis' Outdoor Shop: Carries extensive lines of fishing, hiking and backpacking gear. Sport-Rents provides rentals on everything from fishing to camping equipment. Located on the Town Square. **733-3270.**

Corral West Ranch Wear: Located at 840 W. Broadway, this is one of the least expensive places to buy men's, women's and children's western clothing, hats and boots. **733-0247.**

Sirk Shirts: One of the largest selections of printed t-shirts, sweatshirts, and caps. Located at 24 S. Cache, on the Town Square and in The Mangy Moose Mall, Teton Village. **733-4096.**

RESTAURANTS

You won't have to search for food in Jackson; restaurants are plentiful and most are located near the Town Square or nereby Teton Village. You'll find a wide culinary range to choose from: health foods served from walk-away food stands to four-star restaurants perched on lofty buttes with magnificent vistas. I suggest that you pick up a free copy of the **Jackson Hole Dining Guide** for a complete listing of all the eateries in Jackson Hole. The guide contains sample menus, hours and prices from each restaurant listed. You can find it in most restaurants or with the Wyoming State Information Center, located at 532 N. Cache St.

Expensive: $14-$30 per person, per entree
Moderate: $13-$24 per person, per entree
Inexpensive: $5-$12 per person, per entree

Expensive
Alpenhof Lodge
This casual yet elegant 4-star German Restaurant is one of Jacksons' best. Specializing in veal, beef and game served courteously amid an "Old World" atmosphere. Cocktails, beer and wine. Reservations recommended. Located in Teton Village. **733-3242.**

The Blue Lion

An excellent restaurant serving creative continental cuisine. Specialties include seafood, steaks, veal and vegetarian dishes prepared in a casual, yet elegant atmosphere. Reservations are encouraged. If you dine between 6-6:30, you get 20% off the cost of your meal. Look in one of the free weekly papers for a clip-out coupon. Located at 160 N. Millward. **733-3912.**

The Cadillac Grill

A delightful restaurant serving nouvelle cuisine, with an extensive selection of fish entrees. They also serve fresh pasta, lamb and wild game. Cocktails, beer and wine. Located on the Town Square next to the Cowboy Bar. **733-3279.**

The Granary

Located atop the East Gros Ventre Butte at Spring Creek Resort, the views alone from this 4-star restaurant are worth the visit. Serves an array of international and American cuisine. Cocktails, beer and wine. Reservation suggested on weekends. **733-8833.**

The Strutting Grouse

Winner of the "TRAVEL/Holiday Award for Fine Dining." Offers casual, resort dining and serves local specialties such as sauteed breast of grouse, Wyoming mix grill, trout and more. Varied wine list. Reservations recommended. Located at Jackson Hole Golf and Tennis,

8 miles north of Jackson on Hwy 89 and Gros Ventre junction. **733-7788.**

Moderate
Anthony's Italian Restaurant
A lively, local favorite restaurant that features a large selection of Northern and Southern Italian cuisine. Specialties include veal, chicken, seafood and vegetarian dishes. I especially love the breads and soups that are made fresh daily. Serves beer and wine. Located at 62 S. Glenwood. **733-3717.**

Lame Duck Chinese Restaurant
Serves traditional Chinese, Sushi and Sashimi in a cheerful, airy atmosphere. Dishes include tempura, roast duck, dim sum and vegetarian. No MSG added. Take-out available. One of the best casual Chinese restaurants anywhere. Cocktails. Located at 680 E. Broadway. **733-4311.**

La Chispa
Located downstairs from the Cowboy Bar on the Town Square. La Chispa serves a variety of superb Mexican specialties and offers a wide selection of imported beers. **733-4790.**

The Mangy Moose
Located at Teton Village, your dining experience in the valley would not be complete without a visit to the "Moose." Known for its elaborate rustic design, the Mangy

Moose features steaks, prime rib, chicken and seafood dishes, all complemented with a fresh salad bar. **733-4913.**

JJ's Silver Dollar Bar and Grill

Practically an institution in Jackson Hole, this "good and plenty" restaurant offers blackened rib, steaks, seafood and local game. Breakfasts, lunch and dinner. Located at 50 N. Glenwood, inside the Wort Hotel. **733-2190.**

Tortilla Flats

The southwest meets the northwest at Tortilla Flats. This popular chain originated in Santa Fe, NM and offers a good and authentic sampling of mexican dishes. You can order them as mild or as spicy as you like. Located at the base of Snow King on Snow King Drive.

Inexpensive
The Bunnery

Offering breakfast, lunch and diner, the Bunnery is a local favorite and serves a range of entrees including large fluffy omelettes, fresh soup and salads, deli sandwiches and fresh made baked goods. 130 N. Cache, next to the Teton Theater. **733-5474.**

Shades Cafe

An enchanting and cozy log cabin, Shades is famous for its wonderful homemade sweets, gourmet coffees, espressos, deli-sandwiches, soups and salads. 75 S. King St. **733-2015.**

Bubba's Barbecue
An oasis of savory barbecued or charbroiled beef, chicken and pork sandwiches or platters. Small salad bar. Its homestyle atmosphere and hearty fare make Bubba's a local favorite. Expect a wait during weekends. Serves lunch and dinner. Located on Broadway next to Wendy's. **733-2288.**

Calico Pizza Parlor
Pizza, pasta salads and sandwiches served in a family atmosphere. Located on Teton Village Road. **733-2460.**

Nora's Fish Creek Inn
Locals know a good thing when they see it and Nora's is it for great breakfasts and dinners served in a friendly, rustic atmosphere. Located on Hwy 22 in Wilson. **733-8288.**

Dynamic Health
Serves a delicious array of smoothies, soups, salads, sandwiches and vegetarian dishes. 130 W. Broadway, across from the Wort Hotel. **733-5418.**

Billy Burgers
If you love hamburgers, you've got to try one of these gargantuan creations. The Betty Burger is available for smaller appetites. Other sandwiches are also available. This old-style diner is usually crowded. Next to the Cadillac Grill on the Town Square. **733-3279.**

LODGING

T he valley sees nearly 3 million tourists each year and is well equipped to handle any pocket-book or inclination; from camping grounds to build a cozy fire and raise a humble tent under the stars to 4 diamond luxury resorts offering, golf, tennis, pools and gourmet dining. The following list is a small selection of recommended accommodations in Jackson. For more detailed listings of what's available, contact the **Jackson Visitor's Council** at 1-800-782-0011 or **Jackson Hole Central Reservations** at 1-800-443-6931 or (307) 733-4005.

Room rates vary depending upon the season; summer and winter being the high season to expect higher rates. It is highly advisable to call in advance for reservations and rates during these times. The following rates are based on double occupancy and are the regular summer season rates.

HOTEL/MOTEL

LODGE

Alpenhof Lodge: Located in Teton Village and close to all ski lifts. Balconies, sauna, jacuzzi and pool. The Alpenhof Restaurant offers four star dining and a bar and bistro are also on the premises. Rates are: $86.00-$285.00. Phone: (307) 733-3242; (800) 732-3244.

Antler Motel: 100 units, some offering fireplaces. Hot tub, and cable tv are also available. Located at 43 W. Pearl, near downtown. Rates are: $$66.00-$92.00. Phone: (307) 733-2535; (800) 522-2406.

The Bunkhouse: Dormitory style lodging in the downtown area. Lounge, kitchen, ski lockers and laundry facilities available. $15.00 per bunk with showers at $5.00 per person. 215 N. Cache. Phone: (307) 733-3668.

Days Inn: One of the newer facilities in Jackson offering a free continental breakfast, sauna, jacuzzi, cable and micro/refrig. Located at 1280 W. Broadway. Rates are: $85.00-$129.00. Phone: (307) 733-9010.

49'er Inn: Centrally located, offering rooms with fireplaces, studios or honeymoon suites with whirlpool. Hot tub. Rates are: $68.00-$102.00. Located at 330 W. Pearl. Phone: (307) 733-7550; (800) 451-2980.

Rusty Parrot Lodge: The areas newest facility, nicely decorated and featuring a full complimentary breakfast. Located within walking distance to the Town Square at 175 N. Jackson. Rates are: $115.00-$185.00. Phone: (307) 733- 2000.

Snow King Resort: A full-service resort hotel offering luxury rooms and condominiums. Offers two restaurants and the popular Shady Lady Saloon. Located at the base of Snow King. Rates are: $120.00-$150.00. Phone: (307) 733-5200; (800) 522-KING.

Sojourner Inn: A full service hotel located in Teton Village. Rooms feature beautiful mountain and valley views, queen or king beds, a/c and cable tv. Restaurant, lounge, pool and jacuzzi are also available. Rates are: $59.00-$119.00. Phone: (307) 733-3657; (800) 445-4655.

Spring Creek Resort: A AAA 4-diamond resort located atop the East Gros Ventre, facing the Tetons. Rooms, suites and condominiums are available and all feature beautiful views, fireplaces and goose-down blankets. The resort offers a gourmet restaurant and bar, pool, tennis, hot tub and equestrian center. Rates are: $180.00-$595.00. Phone: (307) 733-8833; (800) 443-6139.

Teton Pines Country Club and Resort: Located in Teton Village, this full service resort offers smartly furnished rooms and condominiums with nice views and a country-club atmosphere. Pool, tennis, golf and dining are also available. Rates are: $195.00-$540.00. Located at 3450 N. Clubhouse Drive. Phone: (307) 733-1005; (800) 238-2223.

Western Hotel: Small facility located in downtown Jackson. All rooms offer tub and shower and cable tv. Pool in summer and whirlpool in winter. Rates are: $68.00-$78.00. Located at 225 S. Glenwood. Phone: (307) 733-3291.

The Wort Hotel: This 4 diamond historical landmark is tastefully decorated and offers nice, recently refurbished rooms. Home to the famous Silver Dollar Bar and Grill and located in the heart of downtown Jackson. Rates are: $145.00-$275.00. Located at 50 W. Glenwood. Phone: (307) 733-2190; (800) 322-2727.

CONDOMINIUMS RENTALS

For large families or groups of people, the most popular and economical way to stay in the valley is in a condo. Your options here are endless, from small studios to spacious 6 bedroom houses. All will come completely furnished, with maid service and most have fireplaces, cable t.v. and telephones. The nicest facilities will offer access to tennis courts, swimming pool and a jacuzzi. Prices vary, but during the high season you can expect to pay between $150 per night for a studio to $600 per night for a 6 bedroom home. The following condominium companies can reserve your condominium for your stay in the valley.

BBC Property Management: 733-6170
Jackson Hole Property Management: 733-7945
Jackson Hole Racquet Club Resort: 733-3990
Spring Creek Resort: 733-8833
Teton Village Property Management: 733-4610
Jackson Hole Central Reservations: (800) 443-6931

BED AND BREAKFASTS

The Jackson Hole area has many good bed-and-breakfasts to choose from.

Fish Creek Bed and Breakfast, located at 2455 Fish Creek Road in Wilson, is a secluded log home on the banks of Fish Creek. It has three rooms, each with a private bath and outside entrance. Rates are $75. (307) 733-2586

Heidelberg Bed and Breakfast

This seasonal B & B is open during the summer months only. Rates are $85.00. Located in Wilson, (307) 733-7820.

Teton Tree House Bed and Breakfast

Mountainside home offers rustic elegance, private baths. Hot tub and fireplace. Rate is $85.00. Located in Wilson. (307) 733-3233.

Wildflower Inn

A lovely log home, offers 5 rooms, each with a private bath. A jacuzzi and solarium overlook the woods and mountains. Rate are $100+. (307) 733-4710.

CAMPING AND RV PARKS

If you are coming to Jackson in the summer and want to save money on accommodations, you're in luck. The valley is full of campgrounds. The Jackson area provides 6 campgrounds, all with RV hook-ups and 4 with tent sites. All of these campgrounds close by the end of October.

Campground	Fee	Dates	Features
A-1 Campground 9 blks W. of Town Square	$13.00	5/15-9/30	Grassy sites, game room.
Astoria Mineral Springs. 17 mi. S of town.	$12.00	5/15-9/15	Hot springs pool, grocery.
B&B Trailer Court 3½ blks SW of town	$11.00+	4/15-10/31	Propane, laundry.
Curtis Canyon 6 mi. E of town	$5.00	6/15-9/10	Goodwin Lake Trailhead
Jackson Hole Campground. City limits.	$12+	5/1-9/30	Laundry, trees, pool, store, fishing.
Wagon Wheel Campground.	$13+	5/1-10/1	Fishing.

For more information, contact Bridger-Teton National Forest, 733-2752.

NIGHTLIFE

Jackson Hole prides itself on keeping visitors entertained, and whether your bent is country-western music, hard rock, swing dancing, movie theaters or a evening of billiards, you'll find something from the vast possibilities to fill your evening hours. Most bars and nightclubs in the area are informal - meaning very casual- and can be found on or very near the Town Square or in nearby Teton Village.

Following is a partial list of Jackson's most popular "hot-spots." For a complete listing of entertainment and acts appearing in the area, check out the After Dark column in the *Jackson Hole Guide* or the Stepping Out section of the *Jackson Hole News*.

Dietrich's Bar and Bistro
Easy listening music in a cozy atmosphere. Located inside the Alpenhof Lodge in Teton Village. No cover. Phone, 733-3242.

J.J's Silver Dollar Bar and Grill
A cozy tradition in Jackson, offering live country-western by single or duo performers on weekends. Home to the famous silver dollar bar-a bar inlaid with over 2,000 silver dollars. No cover. Located inside the historic Wort Hotel, 50 N. Glenwood St., phone 733-2190.

The Mangy Moose Saloon
One of the livelier spots in town offering top name regional and national performers and a dance floor. Reggae, rock, and blues bands most nights of the week, year round. Cover charge. Located in Teton Village. 733-4913.

The Million Dollar Cowboy Bar
A favorite for cowboys and cowboy wanna-be's alike, the Cowboy Bar offers four pool tables and live country music and dancing six nights a week. Burled log beams, stuffed wildlife and saddle-up barstools make this saloon quite different than anything you've probably experienced before. Located on the west side of the Town Square, phone 733-2207.

The Shady Lady Saloon
Located inside the Snow King Resort, this hot-spot attracts a young crowd and offers lots of loud rock-and-roll six nights a week. 733-5200.

The Stagecoach
A favorite, low-key place, the Stagecoach is home to the same country band that has played here since 1969! A small dance floor, three pool tables and a small cafe make for a complete evening of fun, food and entertainment. Located in Wilson, Hwy 22., 733-4407.

The Rancher Bar

Conveniently located on the Town Square, the Rancher is one of Jackson's newest and liveliest editions. The lower level has live entertainment nightly, complemented by a large dance floor. The upper level has a considerably more relaxed atmosphere, with 9 pool tables, televised sporting events and a small bar. 733-3886.

Movie Theaters

There are three movie theaters in Jackson, providing a total of 7 screens. If you want to stay in, there are several very good video rental stores, most provide vcr rentals.

The Teton Theater, 120 N. Cache, tele: 733-6744

Jackson Hole Twin Cinema, on Pearl across from the post office. Tele: 733-4939.

Movieworks, 860 S. Hwy 89, tele: 733-4939.

SKIING

Jackson Hole Ski Resort

Mention the words Jackson Hole to any downhill skier in the country, and you'll have his attention. Tell him you've skied the mountain's steep chutes and bowls, and you'll earn his respect forever. Jackson Hole has a reputation as having some of the best and most challenging runs in the world. It is justified. Half the runs here are in the advanced category. Runs like the infamous Corbett's Coulair and statistics like an unsurpassed vertical drop of 4,139 feet, offers expert skiers some of the most exceptional skiing in the country. The ride up the aerial tram may expose you to some of those extreme, suicidal cliff-jumping scenes you may have only seen in the movies. Yes, they really happen here! The longest expert run is Rendezvous Bowl. It is 4,000 feet long with a 1,630 foot rise.

Now, if all this talk about chutes and double-diamond runs is making you a tad queasy; take heart. This is a big mountain. While Rendezvous is where the mountain gets its reputation for being difficult, the lower mountain, Apres Vous, has some of the best intermediate and beginner runs anywhere. Intermediate skiers can choose from every imaginable terrain and never ski down the same way twice. The longest intermediate trail is 4 miles long and is called the Gros Ventre. The longest beginner run, Eagle's Rest, has only a 300 foot vertical drop and is 2,300 feet long.

The two mountains consist of 25 percent expert runs, 40 percent intermediate runs and 10 percent beginner trails. All of the area within boundaries of the Jackson Hole Ski Resort is considered skiable. This is vast by any standards. The area encompasses 2,500 acres of skiable terrain, 24 miles of groomed trails and several runs that exceed 4 miles in length, providing the most skiing of any resort in North America. The elevation of Rendezvous Mountain is 10,450 feet and adjacent Apres Vous is 8,481 feet. The mountains are serviced by 1 63-passenger aerial tram, 1 quad chairlift, 1 triple chairlift, 5 double chairlifts and 2 surface lifts. Because of magnitude of the two mountains, crowds rarely exist here. If you are going to encounter any crowding, it will be at the aerial tram station, and you shouldn't have to wait any longer than 20 minutes.

While it may seem as though things couldn't possibly get any better here, big changes are on the horizon. During the summer of 1992, the area was purchased by two Wyoming residents, John Resor and John L Kemmerer III, settling a three-year lawsuit between the former owners. While it is unclear what future changes will be made, the new owners do plan to expand the resort.

Getting There

If you need transportation to Teton Village, the easiest and least expensive way to get there is to take the START Bus, only $1 each way. It makes 10-15 runs each day between the hours of 7:00 a.m.-12:00 a.m..

Car rental agencies available at the airport include Avis, Hertz and National. Once in town, it is only another 12 miles to Teton Village.

Ticket Prices

These rates are for chairlifts and poma only. Tram tickets are an additional $2.00 each. All major credit cards are accepted.

$39 Daily Adult
$30 Afternoon Adult
$140 Adult, 4-Day out of 7
$165 Adult, 5 Day out of 7

14 Years & Under/65 and Over
$19 1-Day
$15 Afternoon
$72 4-Day
$85 5-Day

Hours of Operation
Lifts are open 9:00 a.m. to 4:00 p.m. daily, from early December till early April. For more information, call (307) 733-2292.

Ski Schools
The Jackson Hole Ski School, directed by 1964's Olympic gold medalist Pepi Steigler, provides lessons in groups or privately. Some of the more popular classes include 1-full day of group instruction for $40.00, three half-day classes for $70.00, a two hour class for $30.00 or 1 full day of private instruction for $210.00. There is also a special Kinderschule program available for children 6-14.

For snow conditions 24 hours a day, call (307)733-2291.

Snow King
Affectionately known as Jackson's "town hill," Snow King was the first ski area to open in all of Wyoming (in 1939) and one of the first to open in the nation. It looms 7,871 feet directly behind the town of Jackson and offers more than 500 acres of skiable terrain. The mountain offers miles of trails ranging from easy groomed trails to double diamond runs. The longest run is 1 mile in length. Nighttime skiing offers a beautiful way to view Jackson's city lights below.

Getting There
Snow King is located only 7 blocks from the Town Square.

Ticket Prices
$20 Daily Adult
$14 Half Day Adult
$10 Nightskiing

14 Years and Under/65 and Older

$14 1-Day
$8 Half Day
$6 Nightsking

Hours of Operation
Hours are 9:30 to 4:30 daily, from early December to till early April. **(307) 733-5200 or (800) 522-5464**.

Grand Targhee

A recent issue of **Snow Country Magazine** rated Grand Targhee's snow quality as the best in the nation. Many skiers to Targhee would take issue with that statement by saying they believe it to be the best on the planet. Period. Grand Targhee is located on the western side of the Grand Tetons, accessible via Teton Pass.

Here, the views of the magnificent Tetons are as unparalleled as the champagne powder. Targhee sees an annual snowfall of 504 inches-that's 42 feet of the white fluffy stuff! The reason for the prodigious amount of snowfall is because winter storms hit the western side of the Tetons first, then dump whatever is left to the east.

There are actually two mountains located at Grand Targhee. The first mountain is mostly intermediate runs (over 70%) which are groomed every evening. There are numerous black-diamond runs (about 20%), however these runs usually do not require the same level of expertise that similarly rated runs in Jackson Hole require. Even the steepest runs, such as Bad Medicine, the Ugly and Good Medicine, with their deep powder, ski more like intermediate runs than expert level runs. About 10% of the mountain is dedicated to beginner runs.

The second mountain is reserved for snowcat, powder skiing and has over 1,500 acres of unsurpassed powder. Snowcat skiing is 7 days a week and costs $135.00 per day. For more information on Grand Targhee, call **(800) 443-8146**.

Getting There

Grand Targhee is located about 40 miles northwest of Jackson Hole via Teton Pass. The Targhee Express bus makes daily trips to the mountain from Jackson and Teton Village. The buses leave at 7:30 a.m. and return at 6:30

p.m. The price for the roundtrip bus ticket and lift ticket is $35.00.

The Grand Targhee ski resort offers accommodations, restaurants, retail shops, bars, child care and rental shops.

Ticket Prices
$28 Adult Full-Day
$17 Adult Half-Day
$17 Child under 13
$17 Over 65
Free over 70
Hours of Operation
9:30 a.m. to 4:00 p.m.

Ski Schools
Grand Targhee offers several types of skiing instruction: private, group and multi-day lessons are available. The rates are as follows:

Group Lesson (per person):	$18.00
Private Lesson (per hour):	$40.00
Each additional person:	$12.00
3-Hour Private:	$100.00
All day Private:	$160.00

TIP: If you plan to spend several days skiing the slopes of the Tetons, it may well be worth the expense to join the **Jackson Hole Ski Club**. For a $25 annual membership fee, you can receive numerous discounts at nearly 70 different shops and receive half-priced lift tickets. Visit any of the local ski shops for more information or to purchase your membership.

Ski Rentals

If you need to rent or would like to purchase downhill skis while in Jackson, the following ski stores can assist you in either.

▸**Hoback Sports:** 40 SD. Millward St. 733-5335
▸**Jack Dennis Outdoor Shop:** 50 E. Broadway 733-3270
▸**Ski and Sports:** 485 W. Broadway, 733-4449
▸**Teton Village Sports:** Teton Village, 733-2181
▸**Wilderness Sports:** Teton Village, 733-2181

INDEX

- NOTES -

- NOTES -

ABOUT THE AUTHOR

Joy Johnson was born in Cleveland, Ohio and grew up in Michigan and Florida. She moved to the Rockies in 1989 and resides in New Mexico with her husband Tim, their new son Zachariah and cocker spaniel Rufus. She is the author of *The Best Guide to the Canadian Rockies* and has written for several national and international health and fitness and travel magazines and has co-authored four money-management books. However, her love is the great outdoors. She is a member of the Greater Yellowstone Coalition, and when not writing or traveling, she spends her time studying ecology, archeology and anthropology. Hiking is her passion and she is currently working on her next book, *Hiking the Hawaiian Islands*.